The

Wounded Giant

The
Wounded
Giant

*America's Armed Forces
in an Age of Austerity*

Michael O'Hanlon

A Brookings Institution Book

THE PENGUIN PRESS
NEW YORK
2011

THE PENGUIN PRESS
Published by the Penguin Group
Penguin Group(USA) Inc., 375 Hudson Street, New York, New York 10014, U.S.A. •
Penguin Group (Canada), 90 Eglinton Avenue East, Suite 700, Toronto, Ontario,
Canada M4P 2Y3 (a division of Pearson Penguin Canada Inc.) • Penguin
Books Ltd, 80 Strand, London WC2R 0RL, England • Penguin Ireland, 25 St.
Stephen's Green, Dublin 2, Ireland (a division of Penguin Books Ltd) • Penguin
Books Australia Ltd, 250 Camberwell Road, Camberwell, Victoria 3124, Australia
(a division of Pearson Australia Group Pty Ltd) • Penguin Books India Pvt Ltd,
11 Community Centre, Panchsheel Park, New Delhi – 110 017, India • Penguin
Group (NZ), 67 Apollo Drive, Rosedale, Auckland 0632, New Zealand
(a division of Pearson New Zealand Ltd) • Penguin Books (South Africa)
(Pty) Ltd, 24 Sturdee Avenue, Rosebank, Johannesburg 2196, SouthAfrica

Penguin Books Ltd, Registered Offices:
80 Strand, London WC2R 0RL, England

First published in 2011 by The Penguin Press,
a member of Penguin Group (USA) Inc.

Copyright © Michael O'Hanlon, 2011
All rights reserved

ISBN: 978-1-59420-503-3

Book design by Claire Naylon Vaccaro

ALWAYS LEARNING   PEARSON

To my e-generation daughters, Lily and Grace,

and their awesome mom, Cathy

Contents

PREFACE

In a remarkable turnaround from the national security politics of just a decade ago, Democrats and Republicans have recently opted to carry out deep cuts in military spending as a central plank in the nation's new effort to reduce deficits and shore up economic strength. Gone is the hawkish consensus that followed 2001 and led to a near doubling of the defense budget over the next half dozen years, as the nation found itself in not one but two wars. Gone, it might seem, is the predictable Republican tendency to support defense at all costs and always to ensure that GOP political candidates are seen as tougher than their Democratic rivals. Gone is the notion that an incumbent president seeking reelection must avoid any talk of cutting military spending in a time of war.

Now it appears that the military budget may be cut by up to a trillion dollars over a decade, far more than the $400 billion in twelve-year savings that President Obama had proposed in his April 13, 2011, speech that signaled the

White House's full engagement on the deficit issue. That is above and beyond savings that will result naturally, and indeed are already resulting, from troop drawdowns in Iraq and Afghanistan.

And these will be real cuts. The administration's earlier plan, as seen in President Obama's February 2011 budget proposal to Congress for fiscal year 2012, had already taken away most of the growth in the longer-term military budget, reducing it to around 1 percent a year in inflation-adjusted terms. But most military costs rise about 2 percent a year *above inflation*. Perhaps reforms can change that trend, and this book examines several possible ideas for making the attempt. But doing so will be hard, and any progress will be incremental. The 2 percent annual real growth figure reflects a well-established historical tendency and arises from the fact that many areas of defense activity—health care, environmental restoration, weapons purchases, pay for troops and full-time civilians—tend to rise in cost slightly faster than the inflation rate.[1] So it will be necessary to cut forces, weapons, and operations to at least some degree.

Defense cuts are appropriate, even above and beyond the $150 billion or so in annual spending that will naturally go away as forces come home from Iraq and Afghanistan. Our nation is in economic crisis, exacerbated to a large degree by a huge budget deficit and unhealthy level of accumulated debt. This dilemma also constitutes a national security challenge for the United States; no great power can remain great if the economic underpinnings of its strength erode. And to attack the deficit in a serious way, defense must be on the table—just as all other major elements of federal spending, as well as the tax code, must be. Put differently, it is appropriate to factor economic constraints into American military strategy. That is because, from a national security vantage point, the overarching policy goal should be to minimize risk to the nation. And economic weakness is itself a risk.

But before we ask the Pentagon to provide a disproportionate share of spending reductions, as some would counsel, we need to sit back and think. Issues of war and peace are too fundamental to our nation's well-being to be guided by emotional reactions to an economic downturn that, however important, is nonetheless still a temporary phenomenon. We have spent decades building up the best military in the history of the planet and also helping establish an international system of alliances and other security relationships that has prevented another major-power war for almost seventy years. Care is required in changing it. Yes, the defense budget is huge—at nearly $700 billion a year it is one fifth of all government spending, and nearly the equal of all military spending by all other countries on Earth combined.

But it is not large in historic terms as a percentage of our economy; it clocks in at about 4.5 percent of gross domestic product, in contrast to levels around 6 percent under President Reagan and 8 to 10 percent under Johnson, Kennedy, and Eisenhower. And the defense budget is a bargain if the alternative is a higher risk of war.

Nor is America currently a militarized society that somehow needs to reorient its economy or culture. Even if one counts the National Guard and Reserves, only 1 percent of the population is in uniform, compared with more like 2 percent in the latter decades of the Cold War and even higher figures before that. Modern America is more notable for the distance between the average citizen and its all-volunteer armed forces than for any overmilitarization of its society.[2]

Making national budgetary decisions with huge strategic impact cannot be done as an arithmetic exercise. Nor should it be done as part of a grand deficit bargain in which some parties trade away several chips' worth of defense spending in exchange for so many tax cuts or tax increases or entitlement reforms like bargaining chips in a poker game. Yet that seems to be the tendency in Washington today. While it is reasonable, and right, to rethink defense spending in light of our economic straits, we must also ask what our military is for, and what role do we as Americans want to play in the world of the twenty-first century.

This short book, then, aims to spell out the implications of large-scale reductions for American military policy and national security. My bottom line is conditionally supportive of the idea of cutting $350 billion over the next decade—as has already been agreed in the first round of the August 2011 debt deal between President Obama and the Congress. (That cut would actually exceed $400 billion when measured against the Pentagon's previous assumptions or "baseline," because the Pentagon had been planning on some growth above and beyond the inflation rate; by contrast, the $350 billion reduction is measured against a default plan that assumes only enough dollar increase each year to compensate for inflation.) That would translate into a total budget for the Department of Defense, expressed in 2011 dollars, of slightly more than $500 billion a year by mid-decade, in contrast to Reagan-era levels that exceeded $550 billion, current levels today slightly more than $550 billion once war costs are excluded, and Clinton levels around $400 billion.

Some reductions can be found by eliminating pure waste. Some can be found by steps like asking nondeployed military personnel and nonwounded veterans who are using the Department of Defense's health-care system to pay insurance premiums more in line with what the rest of the country considers standard, and also to accept a new military retirement system. The bulk of it will, however, have to be found by cutting real military capability and as a result accepting real additional risk to the country's security. Among other things, the military will become smaller. It might wind up at about 1.4 million full-time troops, in contrast to current levels of about 1.6 million (including mobilized reservists and normal "full-time reservists" who work in administrative jobs), Clinton-era levels around 1.45 million, and Cold War strength that ranged from 2 million to 3.5 million uniformed personnel. The book presents a strategy for making such cuts with the minimum of adverse consequences for the United States and its allies.

But to argue that cuts of this magnitude can be made risk free, as some purport, is not consistent with the realities of the situation. And while there is no exact threshold for crossing into the danger zone, and while calculations relating defense budgets to military power or broader strategic risk are admittedly uncertain, to cut substantially more than the $350 billion would in my judgment be unwise. Certainly anything in excess of a half trillion dollars over a decade should send up major warning flags. Unfortunately, there are budget plans that would do so. Most worrisome is the default plan. As part of the August deficit and debt deal, the new fiscal "supercommittee" is due to present a plan before Thanksgiving for an up-or-down vote by Congress before Christmas. If such a plan is not approved, defense and national security will automatically suffer another $500 billion or so in ten-year cuts, making for a grand total approaching $1 trillion. Spending reductions would have to be very large right away in 2013, probably necessitating layoffs of officers and enlisted personnel who thought the nation had promised them longer-term job security when they first agreed to serve—and when they deployed repeatedly and courageously to the nation's recent wars. Such draconian cuts would jeopardize what I consider irreducible requirements in American defense policy— winding down current wars responsibly, deterring Iran, hedging against a rising China, protecting global sea lanes vital for commerce, attacking terrorists and checking state sponsors of terror, and ensuring a strong all-volunteer military as well as a world-class defense scientific and industrial base. They would also hurt the broader economy at a time when it may still be struggling to emerge from recession. Defense spending is not the most efficient way to stimulate the economy or create jobs. But neither do dramatic cuts to this sector make sense at a time of national economic travail and underemployment.

Behind these specific recommendations is a broader

premise. Not only the United States, but the world in general, benefits from the current international order in which America is the strongest power and helps lead a broader alliance system involving most of the world's other major powers. World peace would not be served by U.S. disarmament or even a trend toward the emergence of multiple, comparable power centers. I do not mean Americans should want to dominate others. Nor should the United States do other countries' fighting for them. But if the United States were to stop playing a global leadership role, competition and conflict would be the likely result. In such a "multipolar" world, countries would often be less confident of their own security, and sometimes inclined to take matters into their own hands by engaging in arms races, building nuclear weapons, or even attacking their neighbors.

We Americans get lots of things wrong, but we usually get around to the right policy after trying all others, as Churchill famously remarked. In the end most peaceful democratic states do not fear us and want to ally with us. As such our power is stabilizing, and desirable. Perhaps someday a world made up just of democracies will, as "democratic peace theory" would predict, be inherently stable on its own, without a strong leader.[3] But the world is not there yet.

Put differently, we have to be careful about cutting defense so much that we weaken our abilities to protect crucial overseas interests. It would be nice if some parts of the world had become less important, or some military missions obsolescent, or some allies much more capable than before. But the world does not offer many such easy options. Helping stabilize the western Pacific region as well as the broader Persian Gulf and Middle East remains very important. Defense plans that would hinder our ability to do so would increase the risks of war in ways that could be enormously costly to the nation and the world. And it is these missions that account for most American defense spending today. We need to be more creative and more efficient in how we protect core interests; doing so will require breaking lots of rice bowls at the Pentagon and, yes, taking some additional risk around the world. But we are not in a position to scale back substantially those interests, because they are integral to global stability.

Some might suggest we could spend less on certain places and potential threats. Take for example Russia. Despite Moscow's prickliness on many issues, it has become more security partner than adversary of the United States. Any threats it might pose to NATO are minimal, even in a world where the challenging Vladimir Putin seems likely to run that country another decade or more. However, our force planning already downplays the possibility of scenarios involving Russia, as it should, so there are no big further savings to reap. Others might suggest we do less in the way of complex humanitarian missions that involve an element of peacekeeping. But these are already tasks that the United States does fairly minimally. The recent Libya mission has gone somewhat better than most such efforts—to the credit of the Obama administration, as well as France and Britain and a couple of smaller Arab states, and most of all to the Libyan opposition itself.[4] But its small scale underscores the extent to which such operations are not a major concern of Pentagon planners even today. That reality was summed up in the unfortunate but revealing phrase used by an anonymous Obama White House staffer that we had "led from behind" in the effort.

Others might think that Korea would offer a more promising case where American security commitments could be reduced. And indeed, in this case, we do still plan for a very substantial U.S military role in any future operation there. It is true that South Korea's military is better than before, while North Korea's is less strong overall. But the last time we tried to ignore the Korean threat, back in 1949 when Secretary of State Dean Acheson infamously declared it beyond America's security perimeter of key overseas interests, what we got was an emboldened North Korea and a full-fledged war. Today, North Korea is ruled by the same fanatical regime as before. And it still has a huge infantry force that would be extremely hard to root out of its bunkers and forests in any future war should, heaven forbid, another one occur. It also has large special forces that would seek to create mayhem wherever they could deploy, including in South Korea, in a future war. Although the conventional military balance on the peninsula may indeed favor the Republic of Korea and the United States, North Korea now probably has nuclear weapons (and its previous stockpile of chemical arms) to complement its other capabilities.[5]

For reasons I develop further in the pages that follow, we would be unwise to draw back from the world or take a big gamble on simply deciding to forgo certain types of military responsibilities. To be sure, we may choose not to carry out the next "war of choice," to use Richard Haass's memorable phrase. We are tired as a nation and need to fix our economy and heal our wounds, not fight abroad again anytime soon.

But we may not always *have* a choice about when and where to fight. In a world with proliferating nuclear arsenals, transnational terrorists, and other threats that can reach out and touch us even from far away, what happens in other regions can affect Americans much more directly than we might prefer. In his retirement ceremony speech of August 31, 2011, the greatest general of his generation,

David Petraeus, warned us that as a nation we do not always get to choose the wars we fight, and it was good advice. Rather than retrench per se, our primary focus in cutting the defense budget should be to look for ways to be more innovative, cost-effective, and brutally efficient in how we prepare for future operations. It is not the time for America to come home from the world.

Admittedly, too, our military is tired. Up to two million committed Americans have been part of the wars since 9/11 in one capacity or another; hundreds of thousands have deployed not once but twice or more to Iraq and Afghanistan; more than six thousand are dead and more than thirty thousand seriously wounded as a result. The toll on military families has been enormous, too. It would be far and away the best thing for this military to be allowed to recuperate, ending the wars and avoiding future ones. But make no mistake about it, today's U.S. military is also the finest fighting force on the planet, beaten up by deployments and war wounds at one level, yet hardened and experienced and battle-tested in ways that make it better than it has ever been in our nation's history. And most of its men and women take rightful pride in what they have accomplished over the last decade, setbacks and all. It would not honor their sacrifice to pull back from our overseas commitments in a way that put all the gains of past years and decades at serious risk.

Military budget cuts should not be, and cannot be, our main means to reducing the deficit. Cutting $350 billion over ten years would entail some risk to America's global interests—and to the prospects for international peace and stability. As such, it can only be justified on national security grounds if the nation's economy is strengthened substantially in the process. Nations with hollow economies cannot be secure indefinitely, so it is legitimate to view the debt as a national security threat, and economic renewal as a national security imperative. However, this idea only works if projected deficits are reduced enough to make a notable difference in America's economic prognosis. And that is only possible if broad-based deficit reduction occurs. As big as the defense budget is, moreover, it is only one of five big components of the federal budget of roughly comparable size—the others being Social Security, Medicare, Medicaid, and domestic "discretionary" programs ranging from science research to infrastructure development to federal support for education. Big defense cuts are only sound policy if they are accompanied by fiscal discipline, including entitlement revisions and tax reforms that reduce spending and increase revenue.

There is no exact point at which defense cuts become excessive and unwise. But make no mistake about it: we will have to cut into muscle, and not just fat or waste, to achieve even the $350 billion ten-year cuts that are now being taken as a given. Such reductions would constitute almost 10 percent of planned spending, above and beyond reductions that will occur as the wars end. This book attempts to develop a plan for accomplishing such reductions without jeopardizing the country's security interests. But I hope to show that even cuts of this size would be risky, and that deeper cuts would be too much. I reach this conclusion not as some superhawk or member of the "military-industrial complex" that Eisenhower warned us about, but as a Democrat, former Peace Corps volunteer, scientist by training, budget specialist by background, and independent scholar. And I agree with deficit hawks that we must look hard, in uncomfortable ways, for means of scaling back. This book contains many such uncomfortable ideas, some my own and many borrowed from others (with appropriate acknowledgment!), as well as my best estimate of associated savings. They do not necessarily represent the definitive comprehensive list of possible changes and reforms in American defense policy. But they do represent the big ideas for cutbacks that strike me as analytically sound at this point.

This book's argument is equally passionate about two points—that the military budget must play a major role in deficit reduction, but also that the process must not go too far and that it must be grounded in a sound national security strategy for the United States.

The
Wounded
Giant

CHAPTER ONE

Introduction

For most Americans, the recent run of trillion-dollar federal deficits has presented serious economic anxiety—taking away homes, evaporating investment portfolios, destroying jobs, and weakening the faith of many in the American dream. For foreign policy strategists, these worries are compounded by a sense that throughout history, great powers with weakening economic foundations cannot stay great powers for long. And as they decline or fall, others generally seek to fill the resulting power vacuum—resulting not only in diminished influence for the former power, but greater instability and risk for the international system on the whole, since war is often the result.

We have seen these worries before in recent times. The

post-Vietnam period was one of substantial malaise in the United States, for example, with military defeat in Indochina exacerbated by the oil shocks and stagflation of the 1970s. Then, after a few good years, things got tough again. By the late 1980s, U.S. GDP growth slowed, budget deficits remained stubbornly high, and other economies outperformed that of the United States. As a result, arguments that "the Cold War is over—and Japan and Germany won" were heard frequently.

Then things got better again, for a while, in the United States. And these U.S. allies encountered their own challenges—Germany in reintegrating its eastern half and then helping establish the viability (and solvency) of the European Union (EU) and euro systems, Japan in dealing with a protracted deflating of its earlier financial bubble combined with demographic challenges that leave its future economic prospects uncertain, at best.

Today, these key allies still have their big problems. On top of that, we are witnessing a period of even greater American economic travails, with much larger fiscal deficits and mediocre national savings rates and an eroding manufacturing base. These are coupled with deep concern that less friendly powers—China in particular, perhaps Russia and others—may be poised to benefit from the relative decline of the United States in specific and the West in general.

Is this true? Given the changing nature of power in international politics, does it even matter the way it once did? And what can we do about it? Most specifically, how can we reduce the national deficit and strengthen our economy without jeopardizing national security through excessive defense and foreign policy spending reductions in the process?[1]

There is no reason to think the rise of China and other emerging powers must be threatening to the United States.[2] There are also powerful arguments that in a world of nuclear weapons, terrorism and civil conflict, infectious diseases, possibly growing threats from biological pathogens, climate change, and overpopulation, the great powers can ill afford the ultracompetitive habits of the past.[3]

But American military power remains a linchpin of stability around the world. Some states do remain menacing, such as Iran and North Korea. Others present uncertain futures given internal turbulence. And for all its impressive attributes, modern China is growing economically—and beefing up its military, including with potent new technologies such as antiship missiles—so fast that it would be a fraught moment for the United States to retrench or lose its verve. Countries that generate huge amounts of economic growth, and see their position improve dramatically vis-à-vis other nations as a result, tend to find it tempting to translate their wealth into military power and to use that power to advance their state interests. Certainly that is a major lesson of history. Maybe things have changed in this modern world. But for all the trends in how countries now interact on the world scene, and for all the changes in modern military technology that some may see as stabilizing, making war unthinkably destructive, there are also aspects to it that may tempt an aggressor to attempt a rapid attack. It is still possible to persuade oneself that surprise, speed, and the lethality of modern weapons can allow quick victory in many situations, for better or for worse.[4]

In regard to China specifically, a strong U.S. military with vigorous presence and engagement in the western Pacific should be seen less as a tool for fighting China than as a way of preserving stability and deterring the outbreak of war in the first place. This is of course the desired outcome of American global military engagement in general, but it is particularly the case in regard to China. Beijing probably does not seek war or military aggrandizement as a core goal of national policy, yet it might be tempted to translate its greater national power into military gains if it perceives a security vacuum to be developing in the region.

Chinese leaders would not have to turn into latter-day Hitlers, Stalins, or Maos to become aggressive. For example, China might feel it could coerce Taiwan into some form of capitulation under certain circumstances. China considers Taiwan a renegade province, every bit as much an inherent part of its nation as Hawaii or Puerto Rico is for the United States, and views any tendencies in Taiwan toward independence as threats to its very territorial cohesion. Under certain circumstances, it could see the use of military force against Taiwan as justifiable, indeed *defensive* in some ways—even as America views Taiwan as a long-standing democratic friend that should not be abandoned. Some serious scholars such as George Washington University Professor Charles Glaser suggest that America rethink its willingness to defend Taiwan with force. But even in the unlikely event that we took Kupchan's advice—which could well lead to Taiwan's pursuing nuclear weapons, and to other U.S. allies doubting America's steadfastness and developing their own as well—the United States would have powerful incentives to retain a strong military posture in the western Pacific to keep that economically dynamic part of the world strategically stable. For such reasons, to say nothing of what truly extremist states like North Korea and Iran may attempt in the years ahead, as well as the ongoing threat of transnational terrorism, there is still a case for strong American military engagement around the world.[5]

One might ask what a country like North Korea or Iran would really do to us at this point in world history. Don't they both know that war with the United States and its allies would be catastrophic? Don't they prefer survival to suicide? Doesn't Iran need revenue from the oil trade, and North Korea economic support from China, to the point where picking an all-out fight with the international community would be unthinkable?

At one level, it is true that neither the Democratic People's Republic of Korea of Kim Jong-il, nor the Iran of the ayatollah and Ahmadinejad, seeks its own demise. But both are risk takers who believe they can play a game of brinkmanship better than we can. Both have pursued nuclear weapons capabilities despite the clear opposition of the international community and their treaty obligations not to do so. North Korea has gone further and shared nuclear technology with other dangerous countries. Both support terrorism—Iran through its proxies in Iraq, Lebanon, and elsewhere, North Korea directly against South Korea (as in 2010, when its navy cold-bloodedly sank a South Korean ship and killed forty-six innocent sailors). Both have stated public positions favoring the annihilation of a country friendly to the United States—South Korea in the case of North Korea, and Israel in the case of Iran. Both already have lots of American blood on their hands, North Korea dating back to the Korean War and Iran in the recent Iraq war, when its weaponry was frequently used by Shia extremists and others to kill American troops as well as many

Iraqis (indeed, that continues, on a lesser scale). None of this means either is likely to wake up and directly attack the United States or its military tomorrow. But both could attack American allies; both could use proxies against American forces in direct strikes; both could create crises to try to extort concessions from the international community, and once started crises are not always easy to contain. This is not a call to preemption against either of the remaining regimes that Bill Clinton called rogue states and George W. Bush called the axis of evil. But it is indeed a warning that we must not let down our guard.

It would be penny wise and pound foolish to jeopardize the general stability of today's international system in an overly assertive effort to reduce the U.S. federal deficit by some specific percentage. Perhaps interstate war among the major powers has become unthinkable today. But that theory has been voiced before in earlier eras, only to be proven wrong by subsequent events, as when Norman Angell's 1913 prediction that economic interlinkages made war unthinkable was invalidated a year later by the outbreak of World War I.[6] Maybe the twentieth century's experiences—huge casualties from the world wars, huge projected casualties in any future war that involved nuclear weapons—have taught mankind the risks of armed conflict. But can we be sure? Even in a world without old-fashioned imperialism, it is hardly inconceivable that new sources of conflict could emerge—over disputed seabed resources, over the uneven effects of climate change on different countries and regions, over nuclear or biological weapons threats that some states perceive other states to be complicit in facilitating.[7] The list goes on.

Today's U.S. defense spending levels are preferable to a major-power war or other serious conflict. Nor do they seem inherently dangerous. The United States already has enough checks on its uses of force, including general casualty aversion as well as a desire to look inward and focus on domestic issues rather than expend resources abroad, that it is probably not necessary to cut defense in order somehow to prevent unwanted operations or harmful defense investments. The United States of modern times is not exactly a peaceful nation, and it is certainly not pacifist. But it is not an imperialistic country either. It has, indeed, fought frequently since the Cold War ended. But its major military operations (Desert Storm, Afghanistan, the overthrow of Saddam) have, respectively, liberated a nation that had been brazenly invaded by a larger neighbor, responded to an aggression that killed 3,000 individuals on American soil, and overthrown one of the worst dictators of modern times. This is hardly the track record of a trigger-happy nation somehow in need of being restrained, even if it is also not a track record that most Americans are eager to repeat anytime soon.

Yes, the United States invaded Iraq without desirable levels of international support or legitimacy. And that war may be seen as unwise by history, even as Iraq currently shows promise of building a better future for its citizens and its region. But if that was the worst thing that modern America could do—invading a country to overthrow one of the world's worst dictators, who was in violation of the terms of the 1991 ceasefire ending Operation Desert Storm, and more than a dozen UN Security Council resolutions— it is easy to see why more than sixty countries still ally with the United States even as they sometimes disagree with it harshly. American power is on balance desirable and stabilizing, and the vast preponderance of other countries know it. And whatever you think of the Iraq war, and the actual decision to wage it, four previous defense secretaries before Donald Rumsfeld and two presidents before George W. Bush all thought we had to be ready for the possibility of conflict in Iraq. Force planners need to anticipate not just what is likely, and desirable, but what is possible about future conflict as well.

To be sure, as a nation we are tired of war. Perhaps we

have also made mistakes in some of our other decisions about the use of force in the past. Beyond Iraq, many Americans would disagree with one or more of the following military operations from our recent history: Vietnam, Lebanon in 1983, Somalia in 1992–93, Bosnia and Kosovo in the late 1990s, and Libya in 2011. If having a smaller military guaranteed that we would avoid mistakes about the use of force, while having enough capability to prevail in smart wars, we would presumably all be for that. But the world doesn't work that way. Moreover, some of the times when we were at our maximal national power, and confidence, as during the Reagan years, we fought relatively less. So it hardly appears that having a strong military makes us more prone to adventurism. George W. Bush himself did not campaign for president on a major pro-defense-spending platform and in fact criticized the state of the military that he inherited from Bill Clinton when on the campaign trail in 2000. Yet it was he who became the author of preemption doctrine after 9/11. Again, there is no obvious correlation between the size, strength, and budget of our military and the proclivity of presidents to use it.

Most of all, being prepared to fight is often the best way to avoid conflict. At times when we have responded to national fatigue by precipitously downsizing our military, as after World War II, we have often encountered unpleasant surprises that required us to fight again, as in the Korean War. We were also unprepared for both world wars, and did not seek them out, yet they happened anyway.

At the same time, it is also true that major American deficit reduction is necessary for the country's long-term strength, and that only by creating a spirit of shared national sacrifice that includes defense cuts can such deficit reduction likely occur on the necessary scale. Former chairman of the Joint Chiefs of Staff Admiral Mike Mullen, former secretary of defense Robert Gates, and Secretary of State Hillary Clinton have all identified U.S. deficit and debt levels as national security threats and they are all surely right.[8] Mullen has called the debt the nation's "biggest security threat."[9] At a political level, too, the American public is likely ready for a period of less assertive foreign policy. The relative desirability of "wars of choice" probably will be seen—and should be seen—as lower in the future than it may have been in the past.[10] The trick is to reflect this sentiment without going too far.

Some pundits toss around simple numbers to make their case that the United States either overspends or underspends on defense. By contrast, I begin from the premise that we cannot deduce whether U.S. defense budgets are too high, or determine appropriate levels, with broad and sweeping arguments about the aggregate size of Pentagon appropriations. Such arguments are common, usually among those with a predetermined agenda of making the defense budget seem either high or low.

Many who wish to defend the magnitude of Pentagon spending often point out that in recent decades its share of the nation's economy has been modest by historical standards. During the 1960s, national defense spending was typically 8 to 9 percent of gross domestic product or GDP, declining to just under 5 percent by the late 1970s. During the Reagan buildup of the 1980s it reached 6 percent of GDP before declining to around 3 percent by the late 1990s after the Cold War ended. Then during the first Bush term, the figure rose and ultimately approached 5 percent of GDP, but is now again headed back down already. Seen in this light, current levels, even including wartime supplemental budgets, seem relatively moderate.[11]

By contrast, those who criticize the Pentagon budget often note that it constitutes almost half of aggregate global military spending.[12] Or they note that recent defense spending levels approaching $700 billion a year exceed the Cold War inflation-adjusted spending average of $450 billion by about 50 percent (when all are expressed in inflation-adjusted 2011 dollars). Or they note that defense spending

FY 1962–2016
Percent

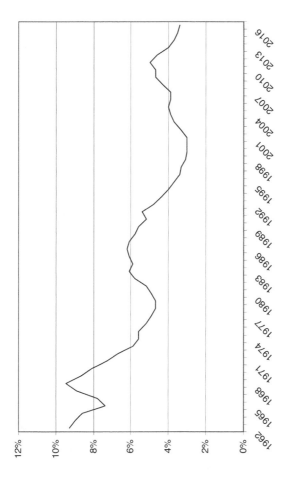

Source: White House Office of Management and Budget, *Historical Tables: Budget of the U.S. Government*, FY2012 (Washington, February 2011), pp. 151–152.

Figures are based on the president's budget request for 2012. Totals prior to 2012 include all war and enacted supplemental funding and include Department of Energy national security spending. Figures for 2012 and beyond do not include estimates of war spending.

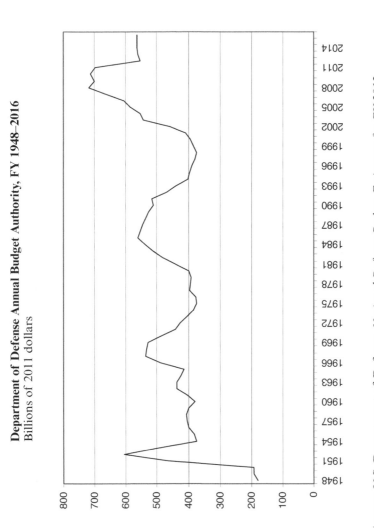

Department of Defense Annual Budget Authority, FY 1948–2016
Billions of 2011 dollars

Source: U.S. Department of Defense, *National Defense Budget Estimates for FY 2012* (Washington, March 2011), pp. 81–86.

Figures are based on the president's budget request for 2012. Totals prior to 2012 include all war and enacted supplemental funding and do not include Department of Energy national security dwarfs the size of America's diplomatic, foreign assistance, and homeland security spending levels, which total around $100 billion a year between them.[13]

These observations are all simultaneously true, and as such they are probably inconclusive in the aggregate. The U.S. defense budget is, and will remain, large relative to the budgets of other countries and relative to other agencies of the American government. Yet at the same time, it is modest as a fraction of the nation's economy in comparison with the Cold War era.

Moreover, American power is nothing to apologize for. A strong United States is good for not only America but international stability, as evidenced by the very small number of interstate wars in recent decades. Deterrence works best, after all, when the deterring state has a clear and decisive advantage over the country that is being deterred. When the balance is close, it is hard to predict historically who will win a given war—indeed, smaller and less expensive forces have often defeated larger ones in the past.[14] It is for this reason that the great Australian strategist Geoffrey Blainey wrote that "The evidence of past wars does not support the respectable theory that an uneven 'balance of power' tends to promote war. If the theory is turned upside down, however, it has some validity."[15] That is, an uneven balance of power can promote peace. Moreover, while ge-

U.S. National Defense Annual Budget Authority, FY 1962–2016
Billions of 2011 dollars

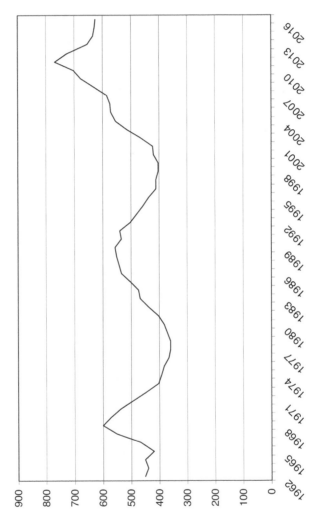

Source: White House Office of Management and Budget, *Historical Tables: Budget of the U.S. Government*, FY2012 (Washington, February 2011), pp. 147–148.

Figures are based on the president's budget request for 2012. Totals prior to 2012 include all war and enacted supplemental funding and include Department of Energy national security spending.

ography helps keep America safe, it works against us in numerous combat scenarios, since the United States would often have to fight far from its own shores and near an enemy's. This makes straight defense budget comparisons potentially misleading.

While informative at one level, these broad defense budget metrics are of little ultimate utility in framing defense policy choices for the future. We must look deeper. Only by carefully examining how defense dollars are spent can we decide if the budget is excessive (or insufficient); the key is to try to identify missions that are not needed, or weapons modernization plans that are too fast and indiscriminate, or war plans that are excessively cautious and conservative. But first, we need to take stock of the state of America's broader security in these early years of the twenty-first century, including the state of its economic security.

CHAPTER TWO

Deficits, Debt, and the Decline of Great Powers

T hroughout history, economic strength has always been a key foundation of military power. To be sure, technological innovation as well as military organizational creativity and tactical cunning have always been central too, as writers from Sun Tzu onward have argued.[1] Political commitment, military courage, and more generally the human element of warfare have been crucial as well, as students of the great Prussian strategist Carl von Clausewitz all understand. But without a strong and prosperous nation behind them, no military leaders or heads of state have been able to keep their countries preeminent in matters of armed conflict for long. Ultimately, the ability to innovate, the capacity to build military forces, and the political will to sustain combat operations require some level of relative prosperity and economic strength.

The basic point that a declining economic power cannot long remain a superpower has been illustrated repeatedly in European history. The Spanish and Austrian Habsburg families/empires, according to historian Paul Kennedy, developed too many military commitments and vulnerable flanks. When they began to weaken relatively in the late seventeenth century, they could not sustain their positions or their interests. Subsequently, the Netherlands also lost its previous illustrious position in the international power rankings because the underlying size and strength of its national economy could not compete ultimately with the likes of France and Britain and Russia.[2]

Britain's period of dominance in the nineteenth century was unnatural in one sense for a country with relatively modest size and population (seventh among the great powers at that time[3]). But in any event, it was not sustainable as the country's relative economic standing dropped dramatically toward the turn of the twentieth century. For example, its estimated share of world manufacturing output fell from more than 30 percent in 1870 to 14 percent in 1913, as Germany rose from roughly 13 to 16 percent and the United States from 23 to 36 percent.[4]

In the post–World War II era, such iron laws of economics worked to the advantage of the United States. Indeed, Soviet economic decline was ultimately a major ally of the United States in bringing the Cold War to an end on terms favorable to the Western world.[5] But even as celebration unfolded at one geostrategic level, anxiety crept in at another. The problem was not just the relative rise of U.S. allies Japan and Germany noted earlier. The fundamental health of the American economy became uncertain, and with it the sustainability of the global economic order that had not only helped win the Cold War but held the Western alliance system together. As Princeton's Robert Gilpin wrote in the late 1980s:[6]

> *The economic era from the end of the Second World War until the 1980s was one of the most remarkable in human history. Following a period of reconstruction in the 1950s, there was an unprecedented rate of economic growth during the decade of the 1960s and the early years of the 1970s. During the approximately forty-year period the world gross national product tripled. International economic interdependence in trade, monetary relations, and foreign investment advanced at an even more rapid pace. . . . [However,] in contrast to the century-long Pax Bri-*

tannica, the era of American hegemony lasted but a few decades. Its demise began with the shift to what would become excessive Keynesian policies and the escalation of the Vietnam War in the 1960s. . . . As had been the case with other declining powers in the past, the United States had indulged itself in over-consumption and underinvestment for too long.

Clearly the demise of the Soviet Union, together with the gradual improvement of the U.S. economy in the 1990s, eased some of these concerns. Japan's economic bubble also burst, and Germany was consumed with the costs of reunification. But by the onset of the twenty-first century, even more significant challenges from even more potentially worrisome competitors appeared in stark relief—and the economic recovery of the 1990s was followed by large deficits, war costs, and then a major financial meltdown.

In recent times, a sense of American economic weakness combined with the rise of other powers, particularly China, has again put declinism into vogue. Samuel Huntington famously argued during the last major period of declinism, the late 1980s, that in fact such thinking is frequent in U.S. history. It has tended to lead to course corrections, ultimately proving the declinists wrong. In other words, because policymakers and the public took fears of

U.S. weakness seriously, they fixed the problems that led to the worries and the decline was typically arrested or even reversed.[7] But are we willing and able to do so still today?[8]

The United States retains many impressive strengths. It is still the world's top economic power, with 20 percent of global GDP.[9] Those who compare this data with the 50 percent share the United States held after World War II as evidence of U.S. decline forget that the postwar period was highly unusual because so many other powers had been so (temporarily) weakened by war. In fact, it was largely U.S. grand strategy that led to the rapid recovery of western European democracies as well as Japan, to say nothing of the rise of new economic powerhouses like South Korea and Taiwan, in the ensuing decades.

Thus, the decline in U.S. GDP as a percentage of the global total should arguably be seen as much a success of American strategy as a weakness or failing. The international institutions that Washington led the way in creating, the foreign aid it provided, and the alliance system it forged made possible economic trends that have generally worked to the United States' advantage.[10] Even in recent years, much of the global growth around the world has been in friendly or neutral countries such as South Korea, Turkey, Brazil, India, Malaysia, and the Philippines. It is not only China that is surging.[11]

As a further benefit of the success of this strategy, most key nations around the world developed a stake in the new order.[12] They also therefore viewed the United States as either friendly, or at worst benign and somewhat necessary. That was not true with the Warsaw Pact or Communist China during much of the Cold War, of course. But the latter relationship was transformed starting with Nixon, and the former bloc ultimately collapsed. Meanwhile the United States led the way in the creation of a security system that, as Steve Walt famously argued, encouraged more "bandwagoning" behavior than the balancing that had typified previous centuries of European power politics.[13]

Even when other major countries disagreed with how Washington handled a specific issue or problem—and they often did, as over Vietnam or nuclear weapons issues or other matters—they did not see the United States as a fundamental threat to their security. As a result, no other major security organization was created to counter American-led alliances. In recent times, the Shanghai Cooperation Organization involving Russia and China may have some motivations along the lines of checking Western influence, but it is not truly a security alliance and carries out no significant military operations or even preparations.

As of today, the United States leads a global alliance system of more than sixty partner states that collectively account for almost 80 percent of global GDP and more than 80 percent of total global military spending between them.[14] (Meanwhile China and Russia have one ally and eight, respectively, according to a recent tally, and these are lukewarm alliances at best.[15]) That U.S.-led system includes the NATO alliance, the system of bilateral alliances in East Asia and the western Pacific, the Rio Pact in Latin America at least at a formal level, and (less formally but quite significantly) American security partnerships with Taiwan, Israel, the Gulf Cooperation Council, and Iraq and Afghanistan. Arguably even India is best seen as part of this system, or at least generally supportive of its logic and its main goals, rather than outside of it. (Pakistan is more complex, and some elements of its intelligence services might even have had a direct hand in insurgent attacks against Americans in Afghanistan, as Admiral Mullen's farewell testimony to Congress on September 22, 2011 underscored.) Among the world's major nations, only China and Russia are essentially outside this somewhat informal but still quite significant network. And America's actual nemeses and potential adversaries—Iran, North Korea, perhaps Venezuela, Syria and Burma and one or two other such countries— collectively account for 1 to 2 percent of global economic output or military power. The geostrategic forces working to the advantage of the United States are extraordinary.

The list of American assets does not end there. As Joseph Nye argues, the country's demographics, including its appeal to immigrants and melting-pot traditions, are more favorable than almost any other large country's.[16] Would-be rivals like China, Russia, and India all have far less favorable demographics. The first is afflicted with over-population, combined with the resulting one-child policy that promises huge economic challenges for the PRC within a generation;[17] the second suffers from underpopulation; the last is already hugely challenged by the size of its population and has not yet adequately slowed its growth.[18] Moreover, as noted before, India hardly seems likely to be a threat to American interests. Delhi may harbor some great-power ambitions, but there are no irredentist territorial issues auguring future problems in dealings with the United States, and in fact few signs of any overly assertive Indian approach to the broader region or world.[19] What great-power rivalries India does possess, notably with China, may in fact tend to drive it toward greater partnership with the United States.

What about trends in areas such as science and education? While some have dwelled on depressing statistics foretelling an American scientific and technological decline, pointing for example to a National Academy of Sciences 2005 report that China was graduating 600,000 engineers a year and India 350,000, to America's 70,000, the reality is not so gloomy. Half or more of China's and India's grads are the equivalent of community college students, or not really engineers at all, as a more precise National Science Foundation study attests.[20] The latest figures suggest that the United States graduates well over 100,000 engineers a year now, with bachelor's degrees or beyond, not even counting foreign students at American universities (who in most cases do in fact stay in the United States and work here after graduation).[21]

When one factors in quality, even the remaining disparity disappears. American universities are still the best in the world, with recent surveys estimating that fifty-eight of the world's top one hundred institutions of higher learning are on U.S. soil.[22] The United States could do a better job of encouraging its foreign student population to remain in this country after graduation, it is true, and it could certainly do a better job of encouraging Americans to study science. But while significant challenges, these are also fixable problems, and they should not be allowed to obscure our strengths.[23]

In terms of research and development spending, the United States still accounts for one third of the global total, easily outdistancing all of Europe combined, and still funding more than twice the research levels of either China or Japan. Other nations are far behind.[24] In terms of U.S. patents, while Americans no longer obtain the outright majority, they do still garner almost half the total despite representing only 5 percent of global population.[25]

U.S. manufacturing is down, as a percentage of the global total overall, it is true. But cutting-edge industries like aerospace, pharmaceuticals, and software development remain robust, with the United States typically producing 20 to 50 percent of global output in these areas of innovation and production.[26] The recent financial crisis has exposed weaknesses in the United States as an investment destination. But there is no obvious preferred alternative as yet among the world's major powers given American strengths—its robust and dependable legal system, its transparent politics, and its traditions of openness to people, investments, goods, ideas, and innovation. It is for reasons such as these that the World Economic Forum still rates the United States fifth in the world in overall competitiveness—and first among major, large powers, with only the small states of Switzerland, Sweden, Singapore, and Finland modestly outscoring it. By comparison, China comes in at position 27, and India, Brazil, Turkey, and Russia at positions 51, 58, 61, and 63 respectively.[27]

But if there are no reasonable grounds for paranoia, nor is there any basis for complacency. The United States has serious weaknesses, as a nation and as an international power. These include first and foremost its budget and trade deficits, which have the effects of weakening investment, surrendering more of the nation's wealth to others, and making the country far less resilient in the face of a future crisis. Prior to the deal of 2011, total debt was headed toward 100 percent of GDP and beyond by decade's end—a figure previously experienced only in the 1940s—with long-term budgetary and demographic trends offering no natural respite from this dilemma. Even with the deals in place, the problem is only mitigated, not resolved.

In fact, the U.S. gross savings rate is now about 11 percent of GDP, half the global average. The nation's net savings rate had declined from around 8 percent a generation ago to 2 percent before the onset of the recent recession.[28] In other words, while America's capital stock was not exactly withering away, it was being sustained and improved only by the grace of foreigners, not by many dollars from U.S. citizens.

Many world-class companies are now appearing in the developing world, with the West often lagging behind.[29] Most major new industrial plants seem to be built abroad. For example, China alone now produces two thirds of the world's photocopiers, microwave ovens, DVD players, and shoes and also makes more steel and cement than anyone else.[30] It is also doing well in some cutting-edge sectors such as advanced solar energy panels.

As of 2010, China produced 18.3 million motor vehicles to Japan's 9.6 million and America's 7.8 million (with Germany fourth at 5.9 million and South Korea fifth at 4.3 million); a decade earlier, it was America in the top spot making 12.8 million vehicles with Japan second at 10.1 million, Germany third at 5.5 million, France fourth at 3.3 million, and South Korea, Spain, and Canada all ahead of China as well.[31] Shipbuilding is now dominated by China as well as South Korea and Japan; the United States barely shows up on global production tables.[32] In another arena of national economic power, the sovereign wealth funds of some countries evidence a longer-term investment attitude, and more concentrated investment muscle, than American companies or funds often muster.[33]

Despite the strength of certain technology sectors in this country, most classic manufacturing industries are in relatively weak shape. Overall manufacturing output as a percentage of GDP declined from 21.2 percent in 1979 to just 11.5 percent three decades later.[34] Unemployment rates are again high, at 9 percent. Rates would be higher still but for the fact that many people have stopped even looking for work. High unemployment may remain a stubborn reality for years, as companies resist hiring until they see a brighter economic future, and as traditional blue-collar jobs continue to fade away.

The country's lower-income classes no longer are making progress economically from generation to generation. For them the American dream of leaving a better future to one's children has stalled, particularly if one focuses on wages. (Workers are getting more compensation than before in the form of more expensive and advanced health care, it is true—but Americans may not appreciate, or even acknowledge, such benefits as much as they do higher wages.) Upward mobility from generation to generation has become very difficult as well.[35] Even if some subgroups, such as female-headed single-parent families, have made some headway, overall poverty levels are worse than in the 1970s— and that was true even before the onset of the great recession in 2008.[36]

Science and technology education levels among the country's public school students are mediocre by global standards—ranking typically in the twenties among forty nations participating in recent surveys. The United States ranks thirty-sixth among all countries in "health and primary education," according to the World Economic Forum.[37] Although the country's engineering talent is a little better than sometimes portrayed, as noted above, it remains true that only 16 percent of American university students get science and engineering degrees, in contrast with levels ranging from 25 to 33 percent in most Western nations and 38 percent in South Korea.[38]

American infrastructure is weakening as newer powers outdistance the United States in everything from high-speed rail to major ports to broadband Internet capacity. Current annual spending on infrastructure is perhaps $20 billion too low simply to maintain existing services, and about $80 billion too low relative to what would be optimal.[39] This is happening at a time when the finances of cities are in greater peril than at any time over the last quarter century. Even if some of the problem is due to the short-term effects of the great recession, the decline in the property values that provide the base for urban services will probably be longer lasting. State budgets are similarly strained.[40]

Surveying such indicators, while the World Economic Forum as noted does rate the United States fifth overall in competitiveness, this is despite a number of serious weaknesses. Looking across various subcategories, the Forum rates the United States only fortieth in the world in the strength of its institutions, fifteenth in the quality of its infrastructure, eighty-seventh in macroeconomic fundamentals, and forty-second in the category described as health and primary education.[41]

America's energy dependence has also grown in absolute terms over the years. About 60 percent of its oil now comes from foreign sources—substantially more than in the past. Its dependence on oil for the transportation sector has barely changed despite various efforts to encourage hybrid vehicles, flex-fuel vehicles, and other innovations.[42]

Finally, while much of America's relative economic decline reflects the emergence of new, impressive, generally democratic, and generally friendly states as noted before, China's rise is of some concern. Because the United States and the People's Republic of China have not yet built a dependably friendly relationship, and because historically rising powers tend to assert themselves on the international stage in ways that often lead to conflict with established powers, China's meteoric ascendance must be watched carefully. As recently as 1980, China did not even rank in the top ten of global economic powers and accounted for no more than 2 percent of global GDP by purchasing power parity metrics. By 2010, it ranked second with 13.6 percent of global GDP. Over that same period, while America's rank of course remained first throughout, its percentage of global production slipped from 25 percent to 20 percent (and as recently as 1960, it accounted for almost 40 percent of global economic production).[43]

China's military spending grew at double-digit percentage rates each year throughout this period too. It reached $70 billion to $75 billion by 2009–10 after being around $40 billion a decade before, according to the estimates of the International Institute for Strategic Studies. Other estimates go higher, reflecting the complexities of accurately gauging expenditures by a country with a much different economic system and less transparency than Western nations. The Pentagon estimated 2010 total military expenditures by China at about $160 billion, more than twice the level estimated for China back in 1999–2000.[44]

Some scholars find this trajectory foreboding. As John Mearsheimer writes, "A wealthy China would not be a status quo power but an aggressive state determined to achieve regional hegemony. This is not because a rich China would have wicked motives, but because the best way for any state to maximize its prospects for survival is to be the hegemon in its region of the world."[45]

I disagree with Mearsheimer's deterministic analysis. For one thing, China's rise is not guaranteed to continue smoothly, for reasons of demographics and environment and other challenges, and a weak China may be more dangerous in many ways than a strong and confident one. Second, in the age of nuclear weapons and powerful conventional forces, the best way for a state to survive is to avoid war in the first place. If China and the United States can reach a modus vivendi in East Asia without war, that is easily the best outcome for both—and there is a good chance that strategists and politicians are smart enough to understand that. Humanity may not be condemned to repeat its past mistakes, and may have learned lessons from a horribly bloody twentieth century.

But Mearsheimer's warning is still important to bear in mind. Certainly numerous countries in the region, including but hardly limited to Japan, are at least somewhat worried about ongoing trends.[46] China is pressuring the United States to stay out of international waters like the Yellow Sea and South China Sea so that it can better dominate these areas, and is throwing its weight around in other ways.[47] The two countries spend a great deal of time and effort on diplomatic engagement with each other, and in the last year or so their military exchanges have stepped up a bit as well.[48] But this process is slow and tough; meanwhile, their forces continue to operate in proximity with the potential for misunderstanding, accidents, and other mishaps. The Chinese military is for the most part not particularly pro-American, and nationalism is strong in the country in other sectors too.[49]

China is investing in new capabilities like antiship cruise and ballistic missiles, cyberstrike capabilities, advanced submarines, advanced fighter jets, satellites, and now an aircraft carrier. These developments are tilting the cross-Strait military balance notably in its favor against Taiwan.[50] Its open-ocean and long-range naval deployments are growing only gradually, but here too there is reason for attentiveness.[51]

The possibility of conflict over Taiwan in particular is real. While China modernizes its forces and realizes that military trends are on its side in the cross-Strait balance, Taiwan has in the recent past unwisely been provocative toward Beijing. Its own nationalism and its own competitive democratic politics sometimes incentivize politicians to do bold things—such as Chen Shui-bian's 2003 hints at a possible referendum on independence. Such an event could have led China to attack the island, since Beijing refuses to tolerate a formally independent Taiwan even if it is prepared to live with an autonomous one for now. It is because of the ongoing possibility of dynamics such as these that Taiwan remains a potential source of U.S.-PRC war. Managing the politics and diplomacy of the situation is the most important key to averting conflict, but sustaining credible American commitment to Taiwan's defense in the event of unprovoked or escalatory attack by China is important as well.[52]

On balance, America is not as dominant as it once was, and it has many weaknesses. But its allies and friends remain very strong, and the Western alliance system is holding together fairly well. China is growing fast but is hardly in a position to dominate its region. American power remains considerable in East Asia as well as other areas. America's strengths in research, education, and high technology more generally are still impressive, and its unique place in the world as a land of opportunity keeps it vibrant and keeps investments flowing in. This mixed picture should lead us to pursue the cause of deficit reduction and economic renewal with a combination of renewed confidence, continued appreciation of the importance of American power, and yet, at the same time, a sense of urgency about changing our ways. That sounds paradoxical, perhaps. But it is the best way to understand the geostrategic and economic position in which the country finds itself today, and to guide us in the crucial policy decisions that lie ahead.

CHAPTER THREE

Deficits, Debt, and a New U.S. Defense Strategy

I n recent years the nation's fiscal situation has verged on
catastrophic. Due to the combined effects of recession
and structural mismatch between revenues and outlays,
the nation's annual deficit has exceeded $1 trillion. That
sounds bad on its face, and the actual reality is even worse.
This is a $1 trillion–plus deficit relative to total revenues of
just over $2 trillion and total spending of $3.5 trillion a
year—in other words, that deficit is enormous in relative
terms as well as absolute terms. We have been borrowing
about a third of the funds needed to sustain the government's various functions over the last three years. Due to the

combined effects, debt held by the public—the best measure of the nation's overall indebtedness—rose from about 40 percent of GDP before the recession to more than 60 percent now.[1]

Meanwhile, that debt is no longer primarily debt held by Americans; half is now held by foreigners.[2] Because of low savings rates by Americans, foreigners also are increasingly important in owning American property and stock equity and other assets. This dynamic has propped up investment as well as research and development activities in the United States. But it means that Americans are accepting a growing foreign role in the economy; indeed, we are bit by bit selling the country to foreigners. And it is only possible if foreigners continue to perceive the United States as a favorable investment haven even in the face of various worrisome indicators.[3]

The August 2011 debt deal between President Obama and the Congress, which mandates some $2 trillion in ten-year deficit reduction, is a step in the right direction in some ways. But the $2 trillion figure is only about half of what is needed to restore sound fiscal fundamentals.[4] It could even be less than that, if the "supercommittee" decides to assume continuation of the Bush-era tax cuts past 2012 (when they are currently due to expire) as its baseline for measuring future deficit reduction.[5] Particularly if tax cuts like those of the Bush years are restored, debt will still likely grow faster than GDP.[6] And near-term steps to avoid a second recession, such as President Obama's September 2011 proposal for nearly half a trillion dollars in additional spending programs and tax cuts, will naturally make the problem worse—even if they may also be necessary under the economic circumstances facing the nation and the global economy.

Such debt levels are debilitating. They can crowd out investment, or at best require foreign largesse to sustain adequate investment levels, leaving the ownership of more and more key national assets in non-American hands. They can make the nation extremely vulnerable to another serious crisis of some type—be it another war, or another major recession, or a flight of investors from American assets that results from a sudden and contagious crisis of confidence in the U.S. economy. High and continued deficits also risk driving debt service levels to very high numbers, especially if and when interest rates again rise. (The Congressional Budget Office [CBO] projects net federal government interest payments rising from $200 billion in 2010 to $800 billion or more in 2020.)[7]

The other problem with the August 2011 deal is its disproportionate emphasis on cuts in some parts of the federal budget over others. Entitlements are largely spared; tax reform is at best deferred; discretionary accounts are most likely to absorb the biggest cuts.

In a dangerous world, there is no reason to think that defense spending should be cut exactly proportionately with the rest of the federal budget—arguably defense spending might need to be protected. On top of that, former secretary Gates already cut, depending on how one measures, some $200 billion to $400 billion in ten-year spending out of the defense program that President Obama inherited. That means the Pentagon had already begun to make its contributions to deficit reduction at a time when the rest of government had not. That said, there is also an argument that, after a decade of wars, Americans may decide to gamble and hope that a more restrictive policy on defense spending is compatible with a stable international environment, in which case defense spending might be cut more than its "share." However, that latter outcome now seems a given, the only question being just how far we push the logic—and push our luck in matters of war and peace. More caution is in order on this score than the country's Washington leadership seems to appreciate at the moment.

A simple way to lay out the parameters for debate is to note the following. Leave aside the 2011 debt deal for the moment and return to the $4 trillion target that Erskine Bowles, former senator Alan Simpson, the rest of their 2010 task force, and many others have endorsed for ten-year deficit reduction. That $4 trillion target assumes extension of some but not all Bush tax cuts. So if all the tax cuts were in fact made permanent, the problem would then get worse and about $6 trillion in subsequent deficit reduction efforts would be needed to achieve the same effect. (By contrast, if none of the tax cuts were continued and other steps like indexing income tax rate brackets for inflation were also put aside, the Bowles-Simpson target would largely be accomplished instantaneously—though few hold out much hope for this outcome.)

So let's go back to the $4 trillion target, and assume that $3 trillion would be in spending reductions. These are huge numbers, but in fact they would not even eliminate the deficit, only bring it down to where growth in the debt would no longer outpace growth in GDP, and as such debt as a percent of GDP would stop growing.[8] So the goal is actually modest when measured up against the magnitude of the challenge.

It is already presumed in the baseline or benchmark for policy that war costs will come down dramatically. The Pentagon's contribution to deficit reduction targets, whatever it may wind up being, will therefore have to come out of its other, "peacetime" costs. The remaining defense costs, what is sometimes called the base budget, make up about 15 percent of federal spending. So if national security accounts were to provide their proportionate share of savings, that would entail about $400 billion to $500 billion in the core or peacetime budget over a decade—roughly what the August 2011 debt deal already mandates. Another way to say it is that annual defense spending, in the steady state, would be almost 10 percent less than previously projected.

The previous projections did allow for very modest growth in Pentagon budgets above and beyond the rate of inflation. But that was no windfall for the Department of Defense. Most defense costs—for personnel, health care, environmental restoration, equipment maintenance, equipment modernization, and the like—go up faster than inflation. In fact, the CBO itself estimates that the average annual defense budget requirement for the next two decades will be about 10 percent greater than 2011 real-dollar levels (factoring war costs out of the equation), with costs for operations, maintenance, and personnel collectively growing 1.5 percent a year faster than inflation over the period.[9] Just to "tread water," the Pentagon needs real budget growth of 1 to 2 percent above the rate of inflation.

The bottom line is this: if one reduces the steady-state annual defense budget by 8 to 10 percent in real, inflation-adjusted dollars over the next decade, as implied by a $350 billion to $500 billion cut in the ten-year defense plan, the cut in force structure will have to be at least 10 percent. It could approach 15 percent. This is a very ambitious target for a military that is already one-third smaller than it was in Cold War times and that remains charged with missions on multiple continents around the world. In the pages that follow, I attempt to show that it may be acceptable—in terms of limiting the dangers that would be entailed by such cutbacks—but it will hardly be risk-free. Were ten-year defense savings approaching $1 trillion to be pursued, as with some deficit reduction proposals, the annual budget would wind up at least 15 percent less than it would have otherwise been, and reductions in actual capability could exceed 20 percent. This would be unwise.

Some might quarrel with this, wondering why 20 percent reductions are not possible for a military that has nearly doubled its real spending since 9/11, from around $400 billion in 2001 to around $700 billion annually a decade later (expressed in 2011 dollars). The answer is that, of that $300 billion in real growth in the annual budget, at least half was for wars that are ending. Of the remaining $125 billion or so, some was eaten up by higher per capita costs in areas such as health care and environmental remediation at Department of Defense facilities. And about half, or some $60 billion to $70 billion in annual spending, was needed to reverse the "procurement holiday" that the country had enjoyed in the 1990s. The Reagan buildup had left us, then, with large stocks of new equipment. By the George W. Bush years, that equipment was aging and in need of replacement, so procurement budgets had to go back up. Unfortunately, we have not yet bought enough new equipment to have the luxury of going back to Clinton-era levels.[10]

As such, some of the proposals on the table in 2011 would reduce net American power below levels of the Clinton years. That would seem excessive, and imprudent, in a world where Iran and China among others appear at least as challenging to the United States as they were in the 1990s (even if Iraq is now less so). The military also has new challenges that were not as acute in the 1990s, such as cybersecurity. It needs stronger and larger special forces than it had before in order to fight extremists directly and to help other states improve their own capacities to do so. In addition, it may need to consider new capabilities like a long-range unmanned naval strike aircraft as well as a new stealth bomber to respond to the strengthening air defenses and long-range strike capabilities of other nations.[11] In pursuing defense budget cuts, it is also important to bear in mind a basic reality: When one reduces combat force structure, not all costs of a given military service come down proportionately. Expenses for research and development, for many intelligence activities, and for some administrative functions are closer to fixed costs than variable ones, so it is hard to look to them for automatic savings just because combat units are reduced by X percent. And savings from things like base closures, while of course possible, often take substantially longer to achieve than the initial cuts in force structure.

It is time to stop tossing around proposals for huge defense budget cuts as if they were chips on a poker table and focus on those possible threats to U.S. interests. Put differently, it is time to focus on strategy, rather than to derive future American defense policy strictly from the framework established in a budget drill, as happened throughout the summer of 2011. To be sure, strategy must always be influenced by budgetary realities, and some level of risk must always be accepted in a world of scarce resources. So it is not inappropriate, or historically unusual, to have a new military strategy motivated by economic constraints. But it would be wrong to let budgetary considerations drive the process completely, as this could lead to false economies—arbitrarily chosen budget targets that could raise the risks of future war with its huge attendant costs.

This discussion leads me to my bottom-line set of assumptions for future defense strategy and budgets: there are certain goals that American national security policy

Department of Defense Discretionary Budget Authority, by Title
Billions of 2011 dollars

Category	2010	2011	2012	2013	2014	2015	2016
Military personnel	157.9	154.4	142.8	142.2	142.7	141.9	140.2
Operations and maintenance	300.9	298.6	204.8	210.4	212.0	214.9	214.2
Procurement	140.1	136.3	113.0	115.6	121.7	123.3	128.1
Research, development, testing, and evaluation	82.8	82.0	75.4	74.5	71.1	67.5	64.7
Military construction	24.1	17.6	13.1	14.1	12.6	12.2	12.3
Family housing	2.5	3.2	1.7	1.5	1.5	1.5	1.6
Revolving and management funds/other	4.9	4.6	2.7	1.2	1.5	1.4	1.3
Total	**713.2**	**696.7**	**553.6**	**559.6**	**563.2**	**562.7**	**562.4**

Source: U.S. Department of Defense, *National Defense Budget Estimates for FY 2012* (Washington, March 2011), pp. 80-86.

Figures are based on the president's budget request for 2012. 2010 and 2011 totals include all war and enacted supplemental funding. All figures are rounded.

simply must accomplish in the years ahead. Failure to do so would jeopardize the nation's security and indeed its long-term economic prospects as well. I would list these goals as follows:

• Responsibly ending the nation's current wars, with sustained modest commitments to Iraq and/or Afghanistan thereafter for a potentially extended period.

• Deterring an assertive Iran in the broader Persian Gulf and Middle East.

• Helping keep confidence and stability in East Asia in the face of major structural change—or, put more bluntly, hedging against a rising China, should it become more assertive and aggressive.

• Keeping a sufficiently robust NATO alliance to provide some basis for global action by a community of democracies and lower whatever remote risks remain of Russia's again becoming disruptive.

• Maintaining enough combat capability to wage one substantial and extended regional war while also carrying out two to three smaller operations at a time, perhaps in support of the ongoing struggle against transnational extremism in the turbulent broader Middle East region. As Bruce Riedel convincingly argues, it is far too soon to declare that struggle over and won despite the death of Osama bin Laden and Anwar al-Awlaki.[12]

• Retaining a reliable, safe nuclear deterrent that is the equal of Russia's and superior to China's, even as the United States pursues lower force levels through arms control.

• Maintaining a strong all-volunteer military.

• Retaining and promoting the world's best scientific and defense industrial base.

• Maintaining some capacity to help stop genocide as part of a coalition, since America's values are part of what help it hold together a large network of nations in common strategic cause.

This is not meant to be an all-inclusive list. The strategic underpinnings of my smaller military posture have their limits. For example, large numbers of forces in Europe and on its nearby waters are not crucial anymore. The improved European security environment is mostly due to the fact that, while Russia is not a completely friendly or benign power, it is not a military threat to the United States or its major allies. Scenarios involving possible Russian attacks on countries like Georgia, as in the 2008 war, are not good candidates for direct American or NATO intervention.[13] Russia is not likely to attempt any attack on a NATO country. Unfortunately, some Russians do continue to view NATO as a threat, underscoring the need for ongoing care by Washington in remaining resolute in support of allies while minimizing any sense among Russians that their interests are being neglected or their security put at risk. As a result, we need to heed Russian views on issues like missile defense (without giving Moscow a veto over deployments), and also keep any future road to NATO membership for states like Ukraine and Georgia very slow. But while the relationship with Russia is not totally friendly, it is better. Headway has been made on issues like the New START arms control treaty, expansion of the northern distribution network for NATO supplies going to Afghanistan, and tighter collective sanctions on Iran.[14] Nor is Russia likely to wind up in some kind of anti-American axis with China, given its rivalries with the PRC.[15] For these reasons too, the idea of actual war between the United States and Russia is not a reasonable basis for American defense planning. Sanctions and diplomacy are more reasonable and appropriate tools for any future serious disagreements that may occur with Moscow. Yet American conventional force planning has already largely moved beyond contingencies involving Russia, so apart from some economies on the nuclear front, there is not that much more to save here.

Some might disagree with my list of irreducible requirements for American security and argue for a more modest list. For example, some might favor a draft, rather than viewing an expensive all-volunteer force as necessary. But the excellence of America's military argues strongly against it. Having a motivated, highly intelligent, hardworking, industrious group of men and women in uniform has been crucial to the nation's success in recent military operations, especially in the information and intelligence eras. Perhaps there could be a debate about obligatory national service, with military service one option within such a program, but that would be a difficult policy to debate and fashion and would take years to implement if it was deemed desirable (which I think it is not). Moreover, some considerable fraction of the military would still have to be professional to provide necessary experience, technical savvy, and leadership.

Others might argue, for example, that we need not focus as intently on the Middle East as before. But in addition to the fact that a number of key American friends are found there, hardly limited to Israel, the Middle East remains the source of more than a quarter of today's global oil production and more than half of world oil reserves.[16] And with America's continued dependence on oil imports, particularly in the transportation sector, it cannot easily afford to see this region's production put at risk. Its own oil imports are mostly from elsewhere, such as Canada and Mexico and Venezuela, but the global oil market is interconnected and interdependent.

Some might favor radical changes to the nation's oil dependence. Fair enough. Let's imagine such a radical change. Perhaps the federal government, starting tomorrow, offered 100 percent rebates on the added costs of plug-in electric cars (which could charge off the electricity grid, effectively shifting their energy source from oil to coal or natural gas or renewable power). Or perhaps it mandated that car companies produce nothing but such plug-ins within, say, five years. Assume further that electricity production could be ramped up accordingly through greater use of other fuels. Either way, it would take another fifteen years, at least, to replace the existing fleet of automobiles.[17] Perhaps defense planners in the 2025 time period will have the option of ignoring the Middle East, but we do not today.

Those who would favor a more radical overhaul and retrenchment of America's role in the world need to recall history before doing so. The defense budget has been reduced even more in previous periods in American history than what is being proposed now, it is true, but consider the consequences. After World War I we retreated to a "Fortress America" approach to the world and, partly as a result, did not do enough to help address the subsequent militarism and aggression of Japan and Germany and the outbreak of World War II. After World War II we rapidly demobilized, and one consequence soon thereafter was tiny, underarmed Task Force Smith's heroic but futile efforts to hold off a North Korean invasion of South Korea in 1950. After Vietnam we downsized and wound up with a "hollow force" that was rampant with drug abusers and unable to handle missions like the attempted Iran hostage operation of 1980.

After the Cold War, the first President Bush and President Clinton reduced the annual budget by $100 billion—the most successful downsizing in our nation's history—but that was against the backdrop of the complete collapse and dissolution of our major foe and rival, the Soviet Union, with its $400 billion a year military budget (more or less). In 2011, it is true that we are winding down smaller wars, and that Osama bin Laden is dead. But global terrorism remains a threat in places like Pakistan and Yemen, Iran remains hostile and inches along toward a nuclear capability, and China's rise promises to change the power architecture of the global system more than anything since America's rise over a century ago.

Or look at it this way. The Clinton-era military was probably roughly appropriate to the challenges of the day, in terms of size and cost and capability—even if casualty aversion and other matters probably kept us from using that military effectively enough against al-Qaeda during parts of the 1990s. Today, the world is at least as dangerous as it was in the 1990s. So perhaps we can go back roughly to Clinton-era capabilities. Perhaps we can even accept a slightly smaller military if we are smart and savvy enough about using new technologies and operational concepts to get more for less. But to cut substantially below where our capabilities were in the 1990s—at a time when Iran is far closer to having the bomb, and when China now has three times the GDP and spends nearly twice what it did at the end of the 1990s on its armed forces—would seem an unwise gamble.[18]

Some would ask America's many allies to do more for their own defense. I agree. Indeed, as other countries gain economic strength, it is both possible and generally appropriate that they build up military capabilities and the confidence to use them. For this reason, the Obama administration was generally correct to let Europe take the lead in Libya, and like its predecessors it is right to sell arms to responsible nations interested in improving their own armed forces. But there are limits to how much of this is desirable in places like the Middle East and East Asia; arms races could result in such regions. Even more to the point, there are limits to how far allies will be willing to go. Most European nations and Japan have strategic cultures that limit their willingness to help protect the global commons in places like the Persian Gulf. They also have economic constraints every bit as binding as our own. Nor is any one of these smaller nations capable of providing the leadership needed to make most large operations succeed—and, more desirably, to make deterrence effective, so that war does not occur in the first place. Only America really has the means for that role.

Thankfully, South Korea, which faces perhaps the most acute threat of any major American ally, does invest substantially in its own defense. But even here, the nature of possible wars on the Korean Peninsula remains so foreboding that it would not make sense for America to pull back from its longstanding ally, as I discuss more later.

The force posture and budget proposal I develop here would cost the United States a bit more than $500 billion a year in 2011 dollars (plus another $15 billion or so in Department of Energy nuclear-weapons-related accounts), by contrast with Clinton-era levels of around $400 billion. But it costs more today to maintain Clinton-era capabilities than it did in the 1990s. Roughly half of the increased costs result from the need to buy more equipment. As noted, in the 1990s we could take a "procurement holiday," having bought so much weaponry in the Reagan years, but equipment stocks are too old to permit another holiday now. The rest of the increase is due to a range of factors—the inexorably rising costs of health care, new expenses in areas like cybersecurity and special operations, and the need to keep military wages competitive and fair. (Veterans Administration costs, however, are not part of the defense budget and do not factor into the core of my analysis—they have doubled over the past decade to more than $100 billion a year, about half in medical costs and the other half in income security as well as benefits like the GI bill.)

So how to take this alternative strategy and devise a military to go along with it, bearing in mind the force structure and global base network that we are starting with? When faced with the need to make unpleasant budget cuts, the Department of Defense's tendency is often to "salami slice" across all services, subservices, and programs. This is often the path of least resistance bureaucratically. But it is also far from optimal.[19] To be sure, a spirit of shared sacrifice helps create teamwork and prevent backbiting and subterfuge. But it fails to protect areas of activity and investment that may be disproportionately important.

If simple salami slicing won't work, neither will singling out one mission or one service to bear the brunt of the pain. American interests are too diverse, and potential combat scenarios too unpredictable, to allow ourselves that luxury. The Air Force and Navy remain particularly important for deterring Iran and for keeping the peace in the western Pacific. The Army and Marine Corps, as we have seen over the last decade, remain crucial when boots are on the ground in stabilization, peacekeeping, counterinsurgency, and counterterrorism missions. Because none of these missions can be dismissed as concerns or possibilities for the United States in the future, it is important to prepare for all of them.

This is not to say that all cuts should be proportional. The Army and Marine Corps, already beginning to downsize as they exit Iraq and now Afghanistan as well, can revert back to their 1990s size after having been enlarged about 15 percent for the wars of the last decade. They have shown they know how to build up fairly fast if need be, and while this logic should not be pushed too far for the reasons listed above, they can probably absorb somewhat larger cuts to their force structure than can the Air Force and Navy.

In my view, while we must not go too far, tactical air forces of the Air Force can be cut about 10 percent themselves, or the equivalent of roughly two fighter wings with some sixty to seventy combat-ready planes plus spares and training aircraft each. That is partly due to the somewhat more modest warfighting posture outlined in this book—"one regional war plus several missions" requires a somewhat less capable force than would two all-out wars.

U.S. Troops Based in Foreign Countries
(as of June 30, 2011)

Country or region	Number of troops	Country or region	Number of troops
Europe		*Sub-Saharan Africa*	
Belgium	1,210	Djibouti	1,722
Germany	45,601	Other	410
Italy	8,647	*Subtotal*	2,132
Portugal	724		
Spain	1,214	*Western Hemisphere*	
Turkey	1,509	Cuba (Guantanamo)	824
United Kingdom	8,622	Other	977
Afloat	370	*Subtotal*	1,801
Other	988		
Subtotal	68,885	Subtotal: all foreign countries, not including war deployments	155,500
Former Soviet Union	155		
East Asia & Pacific		War deployments: all	
Japan	34,362	Iraq and support	91,700
Korea	28,500	Afghanistan and support	111,700
Afloat	8,388		
Other	757		
Subtotal	74,357	Total currently abroad	358,900
North Africa, Near East & South Asia			
Bahrain	1,403		
Afloat	4,899		
Other	2,023		
Subtotal	8,325		

Sources: Department of Defense, "Active Duty Military Personnel Strengths by Regional Area and by Country", Web site (http://siadapp.dmdc.osd.mil/personnel/MILITARY/history/hst1106.pdf). Terri Moon Cronk, "Sharp Emphasizes Need for U.S.-South Korea Alliance", American Forces Press Service, April 6, 2011.

Only countries with at least 500 troops are listed individually. About 12,280 troops were deployed to the wars from the usual bases abroad: 8,350 from Germany, 820 from Italy, 2,350 from Japan and 760 from the United Kingdom. The figures in Iraq are now substantially less.

The Air Force and Navy also retain somewhat overly ambitious weapons modernization plans. So they probably both need to be asked to make greater changes and sacrifices in the weapons acquisition sphere. For example, the Air Force's manned tactical air fleets do not yet adequately acknowledge all the progress made in recent years with drone technologies, on the one hand, and with advanced sensors and munitions on the other. This is another reason, in addition to the recommended change in warfighting strategy, that the Air Force can get by with fewer manned fighters in the future.

Some specific sectors of the military should be cut more than others. Nuclear weapons remain far in excess of the number needed for deterrence. While they do need to be kept safe and reliable, and while the pace at which they are reduced needs to be linked to U.S.-Russia arms control for strategic reasons, our tendency to retain the capability to build back up rapidly in the future is unnecessary.

The Navy's strong preference to avoid rotating crews by airplane to ships that remain deployed overseas for long stretches should be challenged. Its current practice of keeping the same crew on a given ship continuously wastes lots of time when ships are in transit to and from the United States and requires a larger fleet than needed for a given number of overseas deployments, particularly for the surface fleet.

The following chapters focus on developing three basic conceptual frameworks for reducing defense spending and then, subsequently, spelling out their rough fiscal implications:

1. Tougher management, including changes to military compensation policies.
2. Smaller ground forces, returning to Clinton-era levels as Afghanistan winds down, with 10 percent cuts in some Air Force and Navy forces too.
3. More selective modernization efforts.

In rough terms, the first approach might be able to save another $15 billion a year eventually. The second would save $15 billion to $20 billion a year. So would the last, which would build on earlier changes made by Secretary Gates— in early 2009, he canceled vehicle programs within the Army's Future Combat Systems, terminated further production of the F-22 fighter, deferred any development of a new bomber, converted two missile-defense systems from full-bore acquisition programs to just R&D efforts, and canceled the DDG-1000 destroyer. Taken together, therefore, and combined with the cuts already offered by Gates, the three approaches might reach or even exceed $50 billion in annual spending. Allowing for time for these to be phased in, that implies savings of perhaps $350 billion in the ten-year period most commonly used for current budget discussions, as presently already mandated by law—with $500 billion an ambitious goal and the upper end of plausible savings.

Some of these cuts could happen now. Others may have to wait until after the politically charged environment of the 2012 presidential race as well as the most intense phase of the Afghanistan war. Regardless, it is not too soon for the policy debate. In fact it is imperative that both the ongoing Washington debates and the presidential race begin the process of framing and making tough choices for the nation.

CHAPTER FOUR

Tightening Belts
at the Pentagon

When trying to cut the budget, it is appropriate to begin by searching for waste, fraud, and abuse. It is also good politics. Alas, just as there are not that many hugely expensive bridges to nowhere in the domestic discretionary budget, there are not too many $600 toilet seats or gilded hammers in Pentagon accounts. And in fact, one person's waste is often another's important activity or capability. So even in the pursuit of purely unnecessary spending, one encounters rough sledding.[1] But it is still necessary to make the effort and keep at it. Indeed, the changes sketched out here if adopted in full would save about $15 billion a year—though it will prove hard to enact them all at once, as taken together they would leave some troops and particularly some military retirees less well compensated than they are today.

This issue is complex for another, even deeper reason. Because the cases of blatant fraud and abuse are not quite as prevalent or easy to identify and excise as some claim, making management and efficiency improvements in the Department of Defense ultimately requires painful changes in programs that take care of people. Everything from numbers of troops in uniform, to pay raises, to retirement and health care programs has to be scrutinized if big savings are to be found.

Yet this leads to major dilemmas. We are a democracy at war asking young men and women who volunteer for the job to defend us. To be sure, the wars are controversial and not all view them as defensive missions per se. But few would deny that the United States has a special debt to its troops. As one retired four-star general once remarked to me, "Never have we as a nation asked so much of so few for so long." With so many soldiers and Marines in particular having done multiple combat tours over the last decade in Iraq and Afghanistan, it would be not only a mistake, but a moral blight on the rest of us not to take care of them. How can one even begin to talk about curbing their compensation packages and other benefits?

We have the best military in history—and that is not an American birthright, as we know from other periods in our history, like the immediate post-Vietnam days of the so-called hollow force. Rather, it is largely because of the unbelievable quality of our men and women in uniform. We must make military service appealing enough that such individuals continue to join, and remain in, the force. And while making greater use of simulators and the like where possible, we must also continue to train military personnel under realistic conditions to the high standards that have characterized the post-Vietnam American military for a generation.[2]

It is essential to reflect on the quality of today's American military, not simply to praise those who have given so much—though that is certainly important—but also to understand how hard it is to attain such excellence. One small anecdote: I had the honor of helping to interview General David Petraeus for his official military oral history in the summer of 2011 as he prepared to retire and then take over at the CIA. Not all the interviews are yet publicly available, but the last question and answer have nothing classified about them, so I can share them here. I asked him what he thought of today's American military, the organization within which he spent a thirty-seven-year career. He said that it was easy to sum up in a single word—*awesome.*

He then elaborated, describing today's younger officers, noncommissioned officers, and enlisted personnel as bright, full of initiative, innovative, determined, and courageous. He also explained that they are "pentathletes." That is, they can do it all. They know how to fight, to be sure. They know how to protect people, and avoid accidental civilian deaths in the process, which have been remarkably low in our recent wars by any historical standard. They know how to learn local politics and be culturally sensitive too. Indeed, as a former Peace Corps volunteer, I have been struck on my various trips to Iraq and Afghanistan by how military leaders now share the sensibilities and sensitivities that we aspired to in my former organization. These American military leaders are also able to forge alliances with local actors who will work with them to defeat our main enemies, even if some of those allies used to be people shooting at us. In other words, these U.S. leaders are also capable of flexibility, and even of forgiveness. They are extraordinary.

The American military is good largely because it is a learning organization. It does not always get it right at first. We went into Iraq without a serious plan for stabilizing the place once Saddam Hussein was gone; that was largely Secretary of Defense Rumsfeld's fault, as he discouraged attention to such planning, but some key members of the military went along with it at the time. And as Tom Ricks wrote in his bestseller *Fiasco,* some military leaders used too much force early on in Iraq (I thought Ricks sometimes exaggerated his points, but his overall argument was compelling). Yet the military rebounded. It had made a tradition, going back to Vietnam, of training realistically and then carrying out "after action reviews" in which everyone was expected to be self-critical. It does this in wartime extremely well too. But this is only possible because resources are adequate to train realistically and because the military's educational and compensation systems are good enough to attract many of our best and brightest into national service.

One of the heroes of this process was General Ray Odierno, now Army chief of staff. As David Petraeus's main operational commander, he was every bit as much a key part of the surge in Iraq as was Petraeus, yet he was not necessarily fully of the counterinsurgency mind-set at the beginning of the war. Like so many others, he learned and improved over the course of multiple years in Iraq, and became nothing short of a war hero over time. One more vignette: I once asked a Marine Corps general charged with training many of today's Marines how much the service had improved its counterinsurgency capabilities over the last ten years. He said the change was dramatic—on a scale of one to ten, we were maybe a one or two right after 9/11, but up to a six or eight within a few years. He was, in other words, brutally harsh and honest about where we were a decade ago, and while pleased with our progress, still partially unsatisfied with where we are today. That attitude also reflected the constant desire for improvement that typifies today's military leaders. None of these qualities can be lost by the nation as we bring the troops home and cut the budget in coming years.

So change must be pursued cautiously and compassionately. But we should not be daunted in the task. The Department of Defense is not an efficient employer and many of its programs have become more expensive than necessary, or inefficient in how they take care of our troopers, or anachronistic for current times, having been designed decades ago when the challenges of maintaining an excellent military were much different. While the well-being of our troops is paramount, that is *not* the same as saying that every approach currently used to take care of them must be treated as if it were itself a personification of our best and bravest. We need to protect our people, not every one of their current programs or compensation packages.

In doing this, several principles are key to guide future personnel policies. First, our deployed troops and wounded warriors as well as their families must be helped generously; we are doing better and better in this task but still not well enough. Second, we need to incentivize young, technically skilled, and highly motivated people to join and stay in the military. Third, while we cannot and should not ever make military service a lucrative career path per se, we need to be sure that we compensate volunteers risking their lives for their nation reasonably well.

On this last point, the good news is that we tend to do so. The idea that there is a military-civilian pay gap favoring the private sector has become a myth over the years. Private-sector wages, especially for middle-class and blue-collar jobs, have stagnated in recent decades in the United States while military compensation has continued to improve. Moreover, military jobs carry additional benefits above and beyond wages that further favor those in uniform. Statistically, for individuals of a given age and educational background, the American armed forces actually pay substantially *better* today than does the private sector.[3] But that is an average. Some problems exist. Technical experts in areas like computers may still make less in the military. Those who do twenty-year careers in the military get generous retirement packages and those doing less get nothing. Those based at big military facilities can use commissaries and exchanges to get bargains in their shopping, but others have no such benefits. Middle-aged retirees who go on to other jobs, with those generous retirement packages, also get deals on health care that the rest of the country can only dream about in this day and age. Many of these things can and should change. We can actually make military compensation more fair and at least moderately less expensive as a result.

With these principles in mind, the following list of efficiencies and changes at the Pentagon should be seriously pursued:[4]

1. Conduct another round of command closures—and perhaps close a war college or similar DoD educational institution too. Former secretary Gates ordered the closure of Joint Forces Command with possible annual savings in the low hundreds of millions of dollars. The process needs to continue further. Each military service has numerous commands within its own institution. Do the services still need all the component commands they have had in geographic theaters—the Army in Korea, the Navy in Europe—when many of these theaters have seen substantial U.S. military downsizing, and when unified joint commands are also present?[5]

Each service has at least one war college in an era when "jointness" is supposed to be the watchword, and when the size of each service is at least one third less than a quarter century ago. With a smaller military, at least one of the war colleges—in Alabama, Virginia, Pennsylvania, and Rhode Island for the Air Force, Marines, Army, and Navy, respectively—might be closed, with the others being converted to new joint-service institutions. Also, more midcareer officers could go to civilian schools for a year of education (akin to General Petraeus's going to Princeton, as he did in the mid-1980s). Such changes would save at least several hundreds of millions of dollars annually.

2. Implement another round of base closures. As the Cold War was winding down, Congress created a process to close excessive military bases that led to five rounds of reductions and a total cut in capacity exceeding 20 percent. The process was sound, and not unlike the deficit reduction mechanism created by the August 2011 debt deal: A special commission, helped by a professional staff and using economic rather than political criteria, recommends a list of facilities for closure. Congress then votes the package up or down, without the option of revision or amendment given the politics that would intrude if such changes were allowable. There has not been such a round since 2005. It is time, with the military's size stabilizing and indeed going down

a bit further, for this process to resume. Some areas for reduction might include, among others, redundant military research and development facilities.[6]

Since it is possible that future global developments may require at least a temporary increase in the size of the force at some future date, not all the closed facilities should be sold; the government should at least hold on to extra land where it can add more basing on short notice if need be. But the annual costs of operating excess buildings and other facilities cannot be sustained and must be cut. Changes might be considered abroad too, in places such as Germany where despite downsizing in recent decades a large number of facilities remain. A round of comparable magnitude to previous efforts would, once changes are complete, save some $2 billion a year based on estimated savings from earlier closures (in fact, the 2005 round was expected to save more than $3 billion a year according to the Government Accountability Office's November 2009 report on the subject).

3. Increase military compensation more selectively in the future. General pay increases could be held to the rate of inflation, with bonuses of various types used to address specific shortfalls in the force structure. This would keep the faith with an extremely impressive all-volunteer military

at a time when it would be losing certain other benefits, as discussed below, but use any future increases selectively and strategically. The CBO puts annual savings at about $1.5 billion.[7]

4. Consolidate or even eliminate the military exchanges and similar amenities within DoD. These kinds of on-base stores are popular with many military families. But they have unequal benefits, depending on where one is stationed, and they are expensive for the military to run. At a minimum, consolidating them should be within reach, as each service runs its own at considerable inefficiency. CBO estimates that up to $1 billion a year can be saved while still offering many bargains to military families.[8]

5. Rethink, and revamp, military traditions and perquisites such as business jets for many top flag officers. Yes, commanders in the field need their own mobility, but officers running domestic commands do not.

An anecdote from the recent past illustrates the situation. Both the deputy secretary of state and deputy secretary of defense attended the same conference in Colorado. The former flew out, commercial class, by himself. The latter arrived in a military jet with entourage—which was the jet's second trip to the site in as many weeks, since the week before an advance team had come to scout the place out. It is indeed important to protect our key public servants, but the excesses of the deputy secretary of defense's trip were remarkable for a man not in the wartime chain of command and not an iconic or famous public figure. There are dozens of such planes that are superfluous, meaning that at least $200 million a year can be saved by eliminating them.

6. Scale back military bands. Yes, military morale is important and bands help. But gone are the days of slogging months on end through mud, with only field provisions to eat and tents to sleep in. Today's deployed military has, in most cases, DirecTV and hot food and air conditioning—not to say that life is easy abroad, only that the nature of amenities and morale boosters has changed. And where troops in the field do not have such things because of their remote locations or dangerous circumstances, bands will have a hard time venturing in any case. I estimate that roughly $200 million a year can be saved, given that annual costs of bands today exceed $300 million.

7. Increase cost sharing within the military health care program. The TRICARE system provides an extremely good deal for military families. While this has been understandable to a degree, it has arguably gone too far, not only far exceeding the generosity of plans in the civilian economy, but incentivizing excessive use of health care (due to the

low costs). Yet some retirees argue that they were promised free health care for life when joining the military. Well, if they were, it was in many cases a type of health care radically different—and radically cheaper, perhaps by 75 percent or more depending on their age—from what is available today. No one would begrudge wounded warriors the best of care; the issue here, rather, is the cost-sharing system of copayments and enrollment fees for the typical military family, including retiree families. Reforms that retained a generous military health care system but at levels more similar to those in the civilian economy could save $6 billion a year.[9]

8. Change military retirement, as was attempted in the 1980s. The military retirement system is arguably too generous at twenty years of service and not generous enough for those leaving the armed forces sooner. This despite the fact that second careers after the military have become much more common, and military pay relative to private sector pay much better than before. Providing a modest benefit, like matching payments for a 401(k) in the private sector, to the latter group while reducing payments to the former would improve fairness. Higher amounts could be contributed by the government for those who have served in dangerous zones.

This new retirement system would also save money. The Perry-Hadley independent panel that assessed the Pentagon's 2010 Quadrennial Defense Review made this general argument. A recent Defense Business Board study suggests savings that could approach $10 billion a year over the next twenty years. Even if a modified version of the plan only half as ambitious was instituted, and savings accumulated gradually, it is likely that $2 billion to $3 billion a year could be saved over the next decade.[10]

CHAPTER FIVE

A Smaller Ground Combat Force

D uring the Vietnam War, the United States Army's active-duty forces were almost a million and a half soldiers strong. In World War II, the number had approached six million (not counting the Army Air Force or other services).[1] Under Ronald Reagan, the figure was more like 800,000. After reducing that strength when the Cold War ended to less than half a million, and after considering Donald Rumsfeld's ideas in early 2001 to cut even more, the nation built up its standing Army by almost 100,000 troops over the last decade, while modestly increasing the size of the Marine Corps from about 170,000 to 200,000 active-duty Marines as well. We are now on a downward slope again. But how low can we go?

It is easy to see the pros and cons of deeper cutbacks. On the favorable side, we are a nation tired of war, and especially tired of long counterinsurgency missions in distant Asian lands—not for the first time in our history. In addition, we have oceans to protect us from most potential adversaries, and high-technology weapons to try to keep the peace without putting U.S. troops on the ground in foreign countries. On the other hand, in Iraq and Afghanistan over the last decade, we have relearned the lesson that if you want to enhance the stability of a faraway land, you cannot do it with the "shock and awe" of air and missile strikes alone. In addition, if you go in too small, you may only worsen the situation and have to salvage it with larger forces later. Moreover, the size of armies needed to help stabilize such places is partly a function of the size of their populations, not just the quality of our technology or our troops on a person-by-person basis. In a world with more than six billion people, hundreds of millions of whom are still living in turbulent places that could threaten U.S. interests, it is not clear that the American Army can keep getting smaller.

And even if we try simply to avoid manpower-intensive war in the future, we may just fail. We have tried that approach before, deciding that as a nation we were simply done with certain forms of combat. But then we have usually wound up being forced by the course of history to relearn old lessons and re-create old capabilities when our crystal balls proved to be cloudy, and our predictions about the nature of future combat proved wrong. The stakes involved in faraway lands in the age of transnational terrorism and nuclear weapons are too high for us to blithely assume that we've seen the last of complex ground missions in distant places just because we don't happen to like them.

The American military today is indeed the second largest military in the world, after China's. But it is only modestly larger than those of North Korea, India, and Russia. The size of its active-duty Army also only modestly surpasses that of South Korea and Turkey, among others. So as we begin the debate about its future size, we are not exactly beginning with a huge force as a starting point.

Nevertheless, the U.S. military probably can become smaller as the wars in Iraq and Afghanistan wind down. We should not rush into this, and we should not adopt the attitude some advocate that America's main overseas capabilities be reduced principally to Air Force and Navy capabilities. The latter services are formidable and essential. But "standoff" warfare featuring long-range strikes from planes and ships cannot address many of the world's key security challenges today—and possible scenarios in places like Korea and South Asia, discussed further below, that could in fact imperil American security. In the 1990s, advo-

U.S. Military Annual Active Duty Personnel End Strength, 1960-2011

	Total	Army	Navy	Marines	Air Force
1960	2,492,037	877,749	624,895	175,919	813,474
1961	2,552,912	893,323	641,995	185,165	832,429
1962	2,687,690	962,712	662,837	192,049	870,092
1963	2,695,240	961,211	668,626	189,937	875,466
1964	2,690,141	972,546	670,160	189,634	857,801
1965	2,723,800	1,002,427	690,162	198,328	832,883
1966	3,229,209	1,310,144	740,646	280,641	897,778
1967	3,411,931	1,468,754	749,299	299,501	894,377
1968	3,489,588	1,516,973	759,163	308,138	905,314
1969	3,449,271	1,514,223	764,867	311,627	858,554
1970	2,983,868	1,293,276	677,152	246,153	767,287
1971	2,626,785	1,050,425	615,767	204,738	755,855
1972	2,356,301	849,824	593,135	199,624	713,718
1973	2,231,908	791,460	566,653	192,064	681,731
1974	2,157,023	784,128	546,464	192,174	634,257
1975	2,104,795	775,301	532,270	195,683	601,541
1976	2,083,581	782,668	527,781	189,851	583,281
1977	2,074,543	782,246	529,895	191,707	570,695
1978	2,062,404	771,624	530,253	190,815	569,712
1979	2,027,494	758,852	523,937	185,250	559,455
1980	2,050,826	777,036	527,352	188,469	557,969
1981	2,082,897	781,473	540,502	190,620	570,302
1982	2,108,612	780,391	552,996	192,380	582,845
1983	2,123,349	779,643	557,573	194,089	592,044
1984	2,138,157	780,180	564,638	196,214	597,125
1985	2,151,032	780,787	570,705	198,025	601,515
1986	2,169,112	780,980	581,119	198,814	608,199
1987	2,174,217	780,815	586,842	199,525	607,035
1988	2,138,213	771,847	592,570	197,350	576,446
1989	2,130,229	769,741	592,652	196,956	570,880
1990	2,046,144	732,403	581,856	196,652	535,233
1991	1,986,259	710,821	570,966	194,040	510,432
1992	1,807,177	610,450	541,883	184,529	470,315
1993	1,705,103	572,423	509,950	178,379	444,351
1994	1,610,490	541,343	468,662	174,158	426,327
1995	1,518,224	508,559	434,617	174,639	400,409
1996	1,471,722	491,103	416,735	174,883	389,001
1997	1,438,562	491,707	395,564	173,906	377,385
1998	1,406,830	483,880	382,338	173,142	367,470
1999	1,385,703	479,426	373,046	172,641	360,590
2000	1,384,338	482,170	373,193	173,321	355,654
2001	1,385,116	480,801	377,810	172,934	353,571
2002	1,411,634	486,542	383,108	173,733	368,251
2003	1,434,377	499,301	382,235	177,779	375,062
2004	1,426,836	499,543	373,197	177,480	376,616
2005	1,389,394	492,728	362,941	180,029	353,696
2006	1,384,968	505,402	350,197	180,416	348,953
2007	1,379,551	522,017	337,547	186,492	333,495
2008	1,401,757	543,645	332,228	198,505	327,379
2009	1,418,542	553,044	329,304	202,786	333,408
2010	1,430,985	566,045	328,303	202,441	334,196
2011	1,435,450	570,719	328,227	201,466	335,038

Source: Department of Defense, "Military Personnel Statistics" Web site
(http://siadapp.dmdc.osd.mil/personnel/MILITARY/Miltop.htm).

Figures are as of September 30 for each year except 2011, which corresponds to the end of the
fiscal year. Numbers do not include activated reservists or full-time employees of the National Guard
and Reserve. 2011 figures are as of the end of March.

cates of military revolution often argued for such an approach to war, but the subsequent decade proved that for all our progress in sensors and munitions and other military capabilities, we still need forces on the ground to deal with complex insurgencies and other threats.

An emphasis on standoff warfare is sometimes also described as a strategy of "offshore balancing" by which the distant United States steps in with limited amounts of power to shape overseas events, particularly in Eurasia, rather than getting involved directly with its own soldiers and Marines. But offshore balancing is too clever by half. In fact, overseas developments are not so easily nudged in favorable directions; proponents of this approach actually overstate American power. It also suggests a lack of real American commitment. That can embolden adversaries and worry friends to the point where, among other things, they may feel obliged to build up their own nuclear arsenals—as the likes of South Korea, Japan, Taiwan, Turkey, Egypt, and Saudi Arabia might well do absent strong security ties with America.

All that said, we will have to streamline in the years ahead. This is not really for any lack of manpower to people a larger Army and Marine Corps. We have nearly five million young people reaching eighteen every year, and need to recruit only about 200,000 at present for the current military. Although many of the remaining 4.8 million do not qualify for today's force due to their lack of fitness, educational attainment, or other characteristics, ways could be found to make more of them eligible—such as my friend Marshall Rose's idea of *premilitary* fitness camps that could whip out-of-shape young men and women into shape with incentives for positive completion. At present, however, and certainly for as long as the U.S. economy remains weak, availability of manpower will not be our limiting factor. Rather, it is that the expense of having people in uniform has become so great that we must not have more troopers than we need.

As such, once the wars wind down, we should reverse the recent increases in the active forces of the U.S. Army and Marine Corps and return to Clinton and early Bush levels.[2] That would mean roughly 15 percent cuts, relative to current combat force structure—roughly twice the cut currently planned by the services. There was in fact a reasonable amount of bipartisan consensus on those earlier force levels, with defense secretaries Aspin, Perry, Cohen, and Rumsfeld all supporting them over a ten-year period.[3] These reductions in ground forces would not quite achieve 15 percent reductions in costs, as certain nonlinearities exist. New weapons must still be developed regardless of how many will be purchased; weapons unit costs tend to go up when fewer are purchased; some support activities like intelligence do not decline automatically when force structure is cut. But savings would be 10 to 12 percent in the ground forces, or $15 billion to $18 billion in annual spending. Commensurately, Air Force tactical combat forces might be cut 10 percent.

To give a sense of the respective facts and figures, today's U.S. Army has about 550,000 active-duty soldiers. In addition, as of early 2011 data, another 110,000 reservists had been temporarily activated—nearly 80,000 from the National Guard and just over 30,000 from the Army Reserve. The U.S. Marine Corps is about 200,000 strong, with another 5,000 Marine reservists temporarily activated.[4] By contrast, the active Army of 2000 was 472,000 strong and the Marine Corps numbered 170,000.[5] Excluding activated reservists, therefore, making 15 percent personnel cuts would reduce current levels approximately to those of a decade ago.

Today's Army likes to organize its forces and measure its strength more in terms of brigades than the old standard of divisions; there are usually now four brigades to a division, and the former have been turned into units that are independently deployable and operable in the field. Today's ground forces include forty-five brigade combat teams in the active Army as well as twenty-eight in the National

Highlights of Force Structure Recommendations

Category	Current or Planned	Recommended
Active-Duty military personnel	1.6 million (now); 1.5 million (soon)	1.4 million (soon)
Annual Department of Defense budget, 2011 dollars	$555 billion	$500 billion
Army brigade combat teams (active-duty force/National Guard)	45/28	38/24
Army combat aviation brigades (active-duty force/National Guard)	13/8	11/7
Marine Corps active divisions	3	3
Marine Corps combat regiments	15	13
Navy warships (all types)	286	250
Aircraft carriers	11	10
Attack submarines	55	45
Ballistic-missile submarines	14	8
Roll-on/Roll-off strategic sealift	51	51
Airlift/refueling wings (33 planes/wing)	31	31
ICBMs	450	225
Bombers (all types)	150	150
Air force tactical combat wings	17	15
Special operations teams/Ranger battalions	660/3	660/3

Note: Some figures have been rounded.   Main Source: Department of Defense 2010 Quadrennial Defense Review

Guard. The Army also has thirteen combat aviation brigades in the active force and eight in the reserve component. The Marines, organized somewhat differently and using different terminology to describe their main formations, have eleven infantry regiments as well as four artillery regiments.[6] Roughly speaking, a Marine Corps regiment is comparable in size and capability to an Army brigade.

Throughout the 1990s, U.S. ground forces were sized and shaped primarily to maintain a two-war capability. The wars were assumed to begin in fairly rapid succession (though not exactly simultaneously), and then overlap, lasting several months to perhaps a year or two. Three separate administrations—Bush 41, Clinton 42, and Bush 43, and a total of five defense secretaries—Cheney, Aspin, Perry, Cohen, Rumsfeld—endorsed some variant of it. They formalized the logic in the first Bush administration's 1992 "Base Force" concept, the Clinton administration's 1993 "Bottom-Up Review" followed four years later by the first Quadrennial Defense Review, and then Secretary Rumsfeld's own 2001 QDR. These reviews all gave considerable attention to both Iraq and North Korea as plausible adversaries. More generally, though, they postulated that the United States could not predict all future enemies or conflicts, and that there was a strong deterrent logic in being able to handle more than one problem at a time. Otherwise, if engaged in a single war in one place, the United States could be vulnerable to opportunistic adversaries elsewhere.[7] With Saddam Hussein gone, this deterrent logic can be adjusted, a point to which we return below.

In these debates in the dozen years following the Cold War and Desert Storm, most considered actual combat in two places at once unlikely. Few predicted prolonged wars in two places at once. Yet we got exactly that in Iraq and Afghanistan over the last ten years. Of course, many disagreed with the decision to go to war in Iraq in particular. But the basic fact that conflict is unpredictable—that, to quote the old aphorism, "You may not have an interest in war but war may have an interest in you"—endures.

The Obama administration appears to agree; as its 2010 *Quadrennial Defense Review Report* states, after successfully concluding current wars, "In the mid- to long term, U.S. military forces must plan and prepare to prevail in a broad range of operations that may occur in multiple theaters in overlapping time frames. This includes maintaining the ability to prevail against two capable nation-state aggressors. . . ."[8] The Obama QDR is actually somewhat more demanding than the military requirements that guided American planners between 1991 and 2001. It adds a stabilization mission and smaller operations on top of the two-war requirement, though it may be overestimating the capacities of its force structure in doing so.[9]

In my judgment, though, a two-land-war capability is no longer appropriate for the age of austerity. The "one war plus several missions" framework proposed here for sizing combat forces—'one plus two' for short, if the two is understood as two relatively significant efforts—is designed to be a prudent but still modest way to ensure this type of American global role. It is prudent because it provides some additional capability if and when the nation again engages in a major conflict, and because it provides a bit of a combat cushion should that war go less well than initially hoped. It is modest, verging on minimalist, however, because it assumes only one such conflict at a time (despite the experience of the last decade) and because it does not envision major ground wars against the world's major overseas powers on their territories.

More specifically, if there ever was conflict pitting the United States against China or Iran, for example, it is reasonable to assume that the fighting would be in maritime and littoral regions. That is because the most plausible threat that China would pose is to Taiwan, or perhaps to neighboring states over disputed sea and seabed resources, and because the most plausible crisis involving Iran would relate either to its nuclear program or to its machinations in and about the Persian Gulf waterways. It is reasonable for the United States to have the capability for just one ground war at a time as long as it can respond in other ways to other possibly simultaneous and overlapping challenges abroad.

Having such a single major ground-war war capability is somewhat risky, underscoring the risks of even deeper defense cuts than I am outlining here. But it is hardly radical or unprecedented. During the Cold War, American defense posture varied between periods of major ambition—as with the "2½ war" framework of the 1960s that envisioned simultaneous conflicts against the Soviet Union (probably in Europe), China in East Asia, and some smaller foe elsewhere—and somewhat more realistic approaches, as under Nixon, which dropped the requirement to 1½ wars. Nixon's "1 war" would have been conflict in Europe against the Warsaw Pact, a threat that is now gone. His regional war capability, or his "½ war" posture, was therefore similar to what I am proposing here.[10] Nor does this proposal lead to a dramatically smaller ground force. Having the capacity to wage one major regional war with some added degree of insurance should things go wrong, while sustaining two to three protracted if smaller deployments, is only modestly less demanding than fighting two regional wars at once. Unfortunately, today's world does not allow a prudent decision to go to an even less demanding strategic construct or an even smaller force.

This one-war response capability needs to be responsive and highly effective to compensate for its modest size. That fact has implications in areas like strategic transport, discussed further in the next chapter. It also has implications for the National Guard and Reserves. They remain indispensable parts of the total force. They have done well in Iraq and Afghanistan, and merit substantial support in the years ahead—better than they have often received in our nation's past.[11] But they are not able to carry out prompt deployments to crises or conflicts the way that current American security commitments and current deterrence strategy require. As such, we should not move to a "citizens' army" that depends primarily on reservists for the nation's defense.

Translating this new strategy—one war, plus several smaller missions—into force planning should allow for roughly 15 percent cutbacks. Army active-duty brigade combat teams might number about thirty-eight, with the National Guard adding twenty-four more. Combat aviation units might decline to eleven and seven brigades in the active and National Guard forces, respectively. The Marines would give up perhaps two units, resulting in ten infantry and three artillery regiments respectively in their active forces, while keeping their three divisions and three associated Marine Expeditionary Forces. This force would be enough to sustain about twenty combat brigade teams overseas indefinitely, and to surge twenty-five to thirty if need be. If the United States found itself in a major operation, it could and should begin to reverse these cuts immediately, building up larger active ground forces as a hedge against the possibility that the new operation (or additional ones) could prove longer or harder than first anticipated. But that would take some time, roughly two to five years to make a meaningful difference, and as such the peacetime cuts should not go too far.

The above deployment math is based on the principle that active forces should have roughly twice as much time at home as on deployment and that reservists should have five times as much time at home as abroad—even in times of war. That would be enough for the main invasion phase of the kinds of wars assumed throughout 1990s defense planning and the invasion, occupation, and stabilization of Iraq actually carried out in 2003; force packages ranging from fifteen to twenty brigades were generally assumed or used for these missions.[12] So the smaller force could sustain an Iraq-like mission for months or even years while also doing smaller tasks elsewhere.

This capacity falls short of the twenty-two brigades deployed in 2007–8 just to Iraq and Afghanistan, to say nothing of Kosovo or Korea, where additional brigade-sized forces were also present in that time period. If multiple long crises or conflicts occurred in the future, we would have to ratchet force strength back up. Thankfully, the Army and Marine Corps of the last ten years proved they can do this. They added that 15 percent in new capability within about half a decade without any reduction in the excellence of individual units.

Somewhat greater savings—$5 billion to $8 billion more per year—could be realized if the same capability was retained but more of it was located within the Army National Guard. Rather than downsize from forty-five active brigade combat teams and twenty-eight Guard teams to respective figures of thirty-eight and twenty-four, as recommended, one might reduce the active brigades down to just twenty-eight in number for example. The active-duty Army would wind up totaling fewer than 400,000 soldiers with this proposal. The overall U.S. military might compensate by adding not just ten but twenty National Guard brigade combat teams to its force structure, for a total of forty-four. That would keep unchanged the total Army ability to carry out a long-term deployment at acceptable deployment rates for reservists. (In other words, it would add enough additional Guard brigades that their numbers would compensate for the fact that they couldn't be used as often as active units.) This would amount to a major shift in the character of the American Army and would place huge faith in the reserve component. Arguably, the reserve component has proven in recent years that it is up to the task. With twenty-eight active brigades, the Army would still have enough capability to conduct two or three missions while having perhaps fifteen to twenty active-duty brigades ready for quick deployment to a war. However, if a war did begin, the Army would need to move very fast to mobilize a dozen or more Guard brigades to allow them the time needed to train properly so that they could replace the initial response force within a year or so if the operation was not quickly concluded. I am uncomfortable with this degree of reliance on the reserves given the time pressures involved, but it is worth acknowledging that the option does exist.

Some might question whether we even still need a one-war capability. Alas, it is not hard to imagine plausible scenarios. Even if each specific case is unlikely, a number of scenarios cannot be ruled out. What if insurgency in Pakistan began to threaten that country's nuclear arsenal, and the Pakistani army concluded that it needed our help in stabilizing their country? Far-fetched at present, to be sure—but so was the idea of war in Afghanistan if you had asked almost any American strategist in 1995 or 2000. Or perhaps, after another Indo-Pakistani war that reached the nuclear threshold, the international community might be asked to lead a stabilization and trustee mission in Kashmir following a ceasefire—not an appealing prospect to anyone at present, but hard to rule out if a nuclear exchange put the subcontinent on the brink of complete disaster. What if Yemen's turmoil allowed al-Qaeda to set up a major sanctuary there like it did in Afghanistan fifteen years ago? What if North Korea began to implode and both South Korea and the United States felt the need to restore order before the former's estimated nuclear arsenal of perhaps eight bombs wound up in the wrong hands?[13]

Consider the Korea case in more detail. This would not necessarily be a classic war; it could result, for example, from an internal coup or schism within North Korea that destabilized that country and put the security of its nuclear weapons at risk. It could result somewhat inadvertently, from an exchange of gunfire on land or sea that escalated into North Korean long-range artillery and missile attacks on South Korea's close-by capital of Seoul. If the North went down this path, something that its brazen 2010 sinking of the South Korean navy ship *Cheonan* and subsequent attacks on a remote South Korean island that together killed about fifty South Koreans suggest not to be impossible, war might occur out of an escalatory dynamic the two sides lost control over. Certainly the way in which North Korea remains a hypermilitarized state, devoting by far the largest fraction of its national wealth to its military of any country on Earth, while accepting that many of its people wallow in poverty or even starve, should make one worry somewhat.[14] Perhaps Pyongyang might be inclined to try to use that military—in an attempt at brinkmanship or extortion that was foolish to be sure, but that could still prove quite dangerous. It is largely because of such possibilities that the United States should not abandon its South Korean ally, even though that nation is now far stronger than it used to be and stronger than North Korea. The risks of deterrence failure would be too great, given Pyongyang's proclivities to attempt brinkmanship and intimidation. If we did break the alliance, hypothetically speaking, another likely outcome would be South Korean development of a nuclear arsenal, with further erosion of global nonproliferation standards as a result. It is not a risk worth taking now.

It is also possible that if North Korea greatly accelerated its production of nuclear bombs, of which it is believed to now have about eight, or seemed on the verge of selling nuclear materials to a terrorist group, the United States and South Korea might decide to preempt with a limited strike against DPRK nuclear facilities. North Korea might then respond in dramatic fashion. Such a war cannot be ruled out.

Given trends in the military balance over the years, the allies would surely defeat North Korea in such a war and then occupy its country and change its government. North Korea's weaponry is more obsolescent than ever, it faces major fuel and spare parts shortages in training and preparing its forces, and its personnel are undernourished and otherwise underprepared.[15] Yet horrible things could still happen en route to allied victory. The nature of the terrain in Korea means that much of the battle would ultimately be infantry combat. Whatever its other problems, North Korea's rifles still shoot and its soldiers are still indoctrinated with the notion that they must defend their homeland at all costs. North Korea has built up fortifications near the DMZ for half a century that are formidable and could make the task of extricating its forces difficult and bloody. North Korea also has among the world's largest artillery concentrations, and could conduct intense shelling of Seoul in any war without having to move most of its forces at all.

Even nuclear attacks by the North against South Korea, Japan, or American assets could not be dismissed. Sure, outright annihilation of Seoul or Tokyo would make little sense, as the United States could and almost surely would respond in kind, and allied forces would track down the perpetrators of such a heinous crime to the ends of the Earth. Any North Korean nuclear attack on a major allied city would mean certain ultimate overthrow of the offending regime, and almost surely death (or at least lifetime imprisonment) for its leaders once they were found. But the point about nuclear war is that it wouldn't necessarily start that way, and therefore it is not so easy to dismiss out of hand. Perhaps North Korea would try to use one nuclear bomb, out of its probable arsenal of eight or so, against a remote airbase or troop concentration. This could weaken allied defenses in a key sector, while also signaling the North's willingness to escalate further if necessary. It would be a hugely risky move, but not totally inconceivable given previous North Korean actions.

Possible Chinese intervention would have to be guarded against too. To be sure, in the event of another Korean war, Beijing is not going to be eager to come to the military defense of the most fanatical military dictatorship left on the planet. But it also has treaty obligations with the North that may complicate its calculations. And it is going to be worried about any possibility of American encroachment into North Korean lands near its borders. For all these reasons, a Korean war could have broader regional implications—and pose huge threats to great-power peace. This worry requires that Washington and Seoul maintain close consultations with Beijing in any future crisis or conflict. But it also suggests that U.S. and South Korean forces would want to have the capability to win any war against the North quickly and decisively. That would reduce the odds that China would decide to establish a buffer zone in an anarchic North Korea with its own forces in a way that could bring Chinese and allied soldiers into close and tense proximity again. If China insisted on creating such a buffer zone temporarily, by the way, it would be preferable to allow the PRC to do so rather than fight it to prevent such a possibility, in my judgment—to avoid turning this conflict scenario into a possible repeat performance of the first Korean War.

So what does this all add up to, in terms of American force requirements for a possible future Korean contingency? Again, let me underscore my hope that such a horrible war will never occur, and indeed my prediction that it will not. But hope is not a strategy, as Colin Powell liked to say, and in addition often the best way to preserve the peace when dealing with a state like North Korea is to be absolutely clear in one's own resolve and absolutely prepared in military terms. To accomplish this, necessary U.S.

forces would have to be quite substantial. They might focus principally on air and naval capabilities, given South Korea's large and improved army. But they should also involve American ground forces, since a speedy victory would be of the essence, and since as noted the fighting could be quite difficult and manpower intensive. While South Korea is very capable, and has a better military than does North Korea, it would be important to win fast to limit damage to Seoul and to seal off North Korea's borders in order to prevent the smuggling out of nuclear materials.

American ground forces would also be important because American mobile assets (such as the 101st air assault division and Marine amphibious forces) provide capabilities that South Korea does not itself possess in comparable numbers. Perhaps fifteen to twenty brigade-sized forces and eight to ten fighter wings, as well as three to four carrier battle groups, would be employed, as all previous defense reviews of the post–Cold War era have concluded. American forces might not be needed long in any occupation, given South Korea's large capabilities, but could be crucial for a few months.

U.S. forces that were 15 percent smaller than today's would admittedly be hard-pressed in certain other scenarios. They probably could not stabilize a country like Iran, for example. In the unlikely but not impossible event that, due to dramatic Iranian escalation in use of terrorism or weapons of mass destruction, we felt the need to intervene on the ground in that country, a smaller U.S. Army and Marine Corps would be a disadvantage. There is no denying it.

Even in this case, however, we would not lack options. We would retain the ability, even without allied help on the ground, to overthrow a regime such as that in Tehran that carried out a heinous act of aggression or terror against American interests in the future.[16] Such a deterrent could also be useful against any other powerful extremist government with ties to terrorists and nuclear ambitions or capabilities, should it someday take power in another country (above and beyond a current case like North Korea). The force would not be enough to occupy and stabilize a country like Iran thereafter. And leaving it in chaos would hardly be an ideal outcome. But this capability could nonetheless be a meaningful deterrent against Iranian extremism, as we could defeat and largely destroy the Revolutionary Guard and Qods Forces that keep the current extremists in power if it ever became absolutely necessary. That translates into a meaningful deterrent capability—which is of course what we are after, since dissuading the extremists in Tehran from worse behavior in the first place is our real goal. To the extent the international community as a whole then saw the reestablishment of order in Iran as important, it could if desired help provide ground forces in a subsequent coalition to stabilize the place—a job that could require half a million total troops. (Thus, even today's American ground forces would in fact be inadequate to the job of stabilizing Iran, which with 80 million people is three times as populous as either Iraq or Afghanistan.)

For missions like helping stabilize a large collapsing state, perhaps Pakistan or Nigeria, smaller U.S. ground forces could well prove sufficient as part of a coalition. That is, they might suffice if part of the security forces of the state at issue remained intact, or if a broader international coalition of states contributed to the operation.

Consider one of these—the Pakistan scenario—in more detail. Such a scenario is extremely unlikely; for all its challenges, Pakistan does not appear on the verge of collapse. It is also important to underscore, especially in this period of fraught U.S.-Pakistan relations, that any international effort to help Pakistan restore order to its own territory could only be carried out with the full acquiescence, and at the invitation of, its government. That is because there is no scenario I can imagine in which Pakistan's army would entirely melt away, meaning that it would be a force we would have to reckon with and in fact want to work with regardless of circumstances. It is also because the country is so huge that the task would be unthinkably demanding, even with today's military, if the U.S. and international roles were not primarily in support of indigenous efforts. Even independent American writers like me can worry Pakistanis with discussion of such scenarios, and the May 2011 killing of bin Laden only exacerbates the Pakistani sensitivities to any discussion of scenarios that would infringe upon their sovereignty. But we cannot avoid the issue.

Of all the military scenarios that undoubtedly would involve U.S. vital interests, a collapsed Pakistan ranks very high on the list. The combination of Islamic extremists and nuclear weapons in that country is extremely worrisome. Were parts of Pakistan's nuclear arsenal ever to fall into the wrong hands, al-Qaeda could conceivably gain access to a nuclear device with terrifying possible results. The Pakistan collapse scenario appears somewhat unlikely given the country's traditionally moderate officer corps;[17] however, some parts of its military as well as the intelligence services, which created the Taliban and have condoned if not abetted Islamic extremists in Kashmir, are becoming less moderate and less dependable. The country as a whole is sufficiently infiltrated by fundamentalist groups—as the attempted assassinations against President Pervez Musharraf in earlier days, the killing of Benazir Bhutto in 2007, and other evidence make clear—that this terrifying scenario should not be dismissed.[18]

Were Pakistan to collapse, it is unclear what the United States and like-minded states would or should do. As with North Korea, it is highly unlikely that "surgical strikes" to destroy the nuclear weapons could be conducted before extremists could make a grab at them. The United States probably would not know their location—at a minimum, scores of sites controlled by special forces or elite army units would be presumed candidates—and no Pakistani government would likely help external forces with targeting information. The chances of learning the locations would probably be greater than in the North Korean case, given the greater openness of Pakistani society and its ties with the outside world; but U.S.-Pakistani military cooperation, cut off for a decade in the 1990s, is still quite modest, and the likelihood that Washington would be provided such information or otherwise obtain it should be considered small.

If a surgical strike, series of surgical strikes, or commando-style raids were not possible, the only option would be to try to restore order before the weapons could be taken by extremists and transferred to terrorists. The United States and other outside powers might, for example, respond to a request by the Pakistani government to help restore order. Given the embarrassment associated with requesting such outside help, the Pakistani government might delay asking until quite late, thus complicating an already challenging operation. If the international community could act fast enough, it might help defeat an insurrection. Another option would be to protect Pakistan's borders, therefore making it harder to sneak nuclear weapons out of the country, while providing only technical support to the Pakistani armed forces as they tried to quell the insurrection. Given the enormous stakes, the United States would literally have to do anything it could to prevent nuclear weapons from getting into the wrong hands.

Should stabilization efforts be required, the undertaking could be breathtaking in scale. Pakistan is a very large country: its population is over 175 million, or six times Iraq's; its land area is roughly twice that of Iraq; its perimeter is about 50 percent longer in total. Stabilizing a country of this size could easily require several times as many troops as the Iraq mission, and a figure of up to one million is plausible. However, that assumes complete collapse.

Presumably, any chaos within Pakistan would be localized and limited, at least at first. Some fraction of Pakistan's security forces would remain intact, able and willing to help defend their country. Pakistan's military includes more than half a million soldiers, almost 100,000 uniformed air force and navy personnel, another half million reservists, and almost 300,000 gendarmes and Interior Ministry troops.[19] Nevertheless, if some substantial fraction broke off from the military—say, a quarter to a third—and was assisted by extremist militias, it is quite possible the international community would need to deploy 100,000 to 200,000 troops to restore order quickly. The U.S. requirement could be as high as 50,000 to 100,000 ground forces. The smaller force discussed here could handle that.

As noted, another quite worrisome South Asia scenario could involve another Indo-Pakistani crisis leading to war between the two nuclear-armed states over Kashmir, with the potential to destabilize Pakistan in the process. This could result, for example, from a more extremist leader coming to power in Pakistan. Imagine the dangers associated with a country of nearly 200 million with the world's fastest-growing nuclear arsenal, hatred of India as well as America, and claims on land currently controlled by India. I do not suggest that we should create the option of directly attacking such a hypothetical future Pakistan. That said, some scenarios could get pretty hairy—for example, if that future government in Islamabad had ties to extremists and thought about supporting them militarily. Certainly if such a future government was involved directly or indirectly in attacking us, we would need options to respond. These should include the possibility of a naval blockade and scale up from there as necessary, along the lines of the capabilities discussed above regarding Iran.[20]

Even more plausibly, it is easy to see how such an extremist state could take South Asia to the brink of nuclear war by provoking conflict with India. Were that to happen, and perhaps a nuke or two even popped off above an airbase or other such military facility, the world could be faced with the specter of all-out nuclear war in the most densely populated part of the planet. While hostilities continued, even if it would probably avoid taking sides on the ground, the United States might want the option to help India protect itself from missile strikes by Pakistan. It is even possible that the United States might, depending on how the conflict began, consider trying to shoot down *any* missile launched from *either* side at the other, given the huge human and strategic perils associated with nuclear-armed missiles striking the great cities of South Asia. The United States might or might not be able to deploy enough missile defense capabilities to South Asia to make a meaningful difference in any such conflict. But certainly if it had the capacity, one can imagine that it might be prudent to employ it in certain circumstances.

It is also imaginable that, if such a war began and international negotiators were trying to figure out how to end it, an international force could be invited to help stabilize the situation for a number of years. India in particular would be adamantly against this idea today, but things could change if war broke out and such a force seemed the only way to reverse the momentum toward all-out nuclear war in South Asia. American forces would quite likely need to play a key role, as others do not have the capacity or political confidence to handle the mission on their own.[21]

With forty-nine brigade equivalents in its active Army and Marine Corps forces, and another twenty-four Army National Guard brigades, the United States could handle a combination of challenges reasonably well. Suppose for example that in the year 2015, it had one brigade in a stabilization mission in Yemen, two brigades still in Afghanistan, and two brigades as part of a multinational peace operation in Kashmir. Suppose then that another war in Korea breaks out, requiring a peak of twenty U.S. combat brigades for the first three months, after which fifteen are needed for another year or more. That is within the capacity of the smaller force—though just barely. Specifically, after the initial surge to Korea, the United States would by these assumptions settle back into a set of missions that required twenty brigade equivalents in all for some period of a year or more. The ground forces designed here would be up to the task.

Of course, with different assumptions it would be possible to generate different force requirements, making my recommended force look too small or alternatively bigger than necessary. But the demands assumed above are not capricious. They are based on real war plans for Korea, and very plausible assumptions about two to three possible missions elsewhere. And they do not take the U.S. military too far below levels that have recently been necessary for Iraq and Afghanistan, given that recent history should remind us of any overconfidence about predicting the end of the era of major ground operations abroad.

One final important point demands attention in this analysis of scenarios around the world: what is the role of U.S. allies in each of them? The fact that America has so many allies is extremely important—it signals that most other major powers around the world are at least loosely aligned with America on major strategic matters. They may not choose to be with us on every mission, as the Iraq experience proves. But when America is directly threatened, as in 9/11, the Western alliance system is rather extraordinary. This has been evidenced in Afghanistan, where through thick and thin, even at the ten-year mark of the war, the coalition still includes combat forces from some forty-eight countries.

Yet how much help do these allies tend to provide? Here the answer is, and will remain, more nuanced. The other forty-seven nations in Afghanistan have, in 2011, collectively provided less than one third of all foreign forces;

the United States by itself provided more than two thirds. Still, more than forty thousand forces is nothing to trivialize.

The allies have taken the lead in Libya in 2011. But this may be the exception that proves the rule—the mission that they led was a very limited air campaign in a nearby country. The French also helped depose a brutal dictator in Ivory Coast in 2011, and some European and Asian allies as well as other nations continue to slog away in peace operations in places such as Congo and Lebanon. The Australians tend to be dependable partners, Canada did a great deal in Afghanistan and took heavy losses before finally pulling out its combat forces in 2011, and over in Asia, the Japanese are also showing some greater assertiveness as their concerns about China's rise lead to more muscular naval operations by Tokyo.

For future American strategy, however, we should keep our expectations in check. Overall, the allies are not stepping up their game to new levels. Any hope that the election of Barack Obama with his more inclusive and multilateral style of leadership would lead them to do so are proving generally unwarranted. NATO defense spending is slipping downward, from a starting point that was not very impressive to begin with. The allies were collectively more capable in the 1990s, when they contributed most of the ground troops that NATO deployed to the Balkans, than they are now.

The fraction of the NATO allies' GDP spent on their armed forces has declined to about 1.7 percent as of 2009, well under half the U.S. figure. That is a reduction from NATO's earlier figure of 2.2 percent in 2000 and about 2.5 percent in 1990.[22] Secretary Gates accordingly warned of the possibility of a two-tier alliance before leaving office in 2011.[23] Yet NATO is also an excellent insurance policy should trouble loom in the future with China, Russia, or another power. As a time-tested community of democracies sharing common values and historical experiences, the alliance offers America a very useful anchor in sometimes unstable Eurasian waters.

The bottom line is this: When allies feel directly threatened, as Japan and South Korea sometimes do now, they will pony up at least to a degree. South Korea in particular can be counted on to provide many air and naval forces, and most of the needed ground forces, for any major operation on the peninsula in the future. (South Korea is less enthusiastic about being pulled into an anti-China coalition, and Washington needs to watch not only the substance but even the tone of its comments on this subject.[24]) Taiwan would surely do what it could to help fend off a possible Chinese attack, not leaving the whole job to the American military in the event that terrible scenario someday unfolds, though it is probably underspending on its military (see below for more on this). Many if not most NATO forces will be careful in drawing down troops from Afghanistan, making cuts roughly in proportion to those of the United States over the next two to three years.

In the Persian Gulf, both Saudi Arabia and the United Arab Emirates have impressive air forces, with at least one hundred top-of-the-line aircraft each. Both countries could certainly help provide patrols over their own airspace as defensive measures in a future conflict. If they had already been directly attacked by Iran, they might also be willing to carry out counterstrikes against Iranian land or sea targets. But again there are limits. Neither country trains that intensively on a frequent basis with the United States to the point where combined combat operations in limited geographic spaces would be an entirely comfortable proposition. To put it more bluntly, we might have a number of friendly-fire incidents and shoot down each other's planes. Even more concerning, if Iran had not actually attacked their territories, Saudi Arabia and the UAE might prefer to avoid striking Iran themselves first—since once the hostilities ended, they would have to coexist in the same neighborhood again. For that and other reasons, it is not completely clear that we could count on regional allies to do more than the very important but still limited task of protecting their own airspace. We could hope for more, but should not count on it for force-planning purposes. A similar logic would apply to Japan in the event of any war against China over Taiwan.

Britain can be counted on for a brigade or two—five thousand to ten thousand troops, perhaps—for most major operations that the United States might consider in the future. Some new NATO allies like Poland and Romania, and some aspirants like Georgia, will try to help where they can, largely to solidify ties to America that they consider crucial for their security. The allies also *may* have enough collective capacity, and political will, to share responsibility for humanitarian and peace operations in the future, though here frankly the record of the entire Western world including the United States is patchy at best. Numerous countries will contribute modestly to limited and low-risk missions like the counterpiracy patrols off the coast of Somalia. If future naval operations are needed perhaps to monitor or enforce future sanctions on Iran, and if we are then lucky, we may get a few allies to participate. Maybe. But that is about as far as it will go.

The bottom line is that the United States need not, and should not, accept primary responsibility for future military operations of a humanitarian nature, and it should not have to play a preponderant role in most future peace operations. But even if it will not have to be the world's policeman, it will to an extent have to remain the world's main security guarantor, or at least the lead player in future coalitions designed to carry out that role—providing heavy combat forces for the most serious scenarios, largely on its own among the Western powers. In specific cases, we can always hope for more help. But for planning purposes, we had best not count on too much of it, beyond what a couple key allies like Britain and South Korea could be expected to provide in substantial amounts for certain scenarios.

CHAPTER SIX

Global Basing and Global Presence

America's military may not be huge, but it is everywhere, and it is busy. Try to find a member of the military who has not deployed over the last decade; there aren't many. Former deputy secretary of defense William Lynn stated recently that two million Americans had served abroad in combat-related missions over the last ten years, and that is hardly the end of it, as the U.S. military presence is also robust in East Asia and Europe and other places where there has been no recent war.

To form a mental map of where America routinely deploys force abroad, think of it this way. One major concentration is in Europe, centered on Germany but also with substantial numbers of forces in the United Kingdom and Italy, and more modest presence in a few more countries like Spain. A second major capability is in the dynamic East Asia region, with large standing American forces in both Korea and Japan and large numbers of ships routinely on station in the western Pacific as well. The third main area of focus is of course in the broader "Central Command" region. GIs in Iraq have almost all now come home, but the United States retains numerous capabilities throughout the Persian Gulf region, on land and at sea. And of course America still has very large numbers of troopers engaged in combat operations and stabilization activities in Afghanistan. These big force laydowns in eight or ten locations around the globe are complemented by smaller numbers of troops in a large number of additional places on every continent except Antarctica, sometimes maintaining a durable presence and sometimes rotating through to carry out exercises or handle crises or just show the flag.

In playing its worldwide military role, the United States has more than sixty formal allies or other close security partners with whom it teams in one way or another. Its national security strategy for decades has viewed virtually the entirety of Eurasia's coastal regions as an important American national security interest. South Asia and Southeast Asia have sometimes been within this perimeter, sometimes not, but Europe, the Middle East/Persian Gulf region, and East Asia have consistently factored critically into the U.S. national security equation. And today's American military is sized and built not just for hypothetical conflict scenarios, not just for the ongoing mission in Afghanistan, but also for sustained deployment and presence in much of that region.

This sounds enormously ambitious and costly. In some ways, it surely is. Defending America's own territory would surely be feasible at far less cost, with far fewer forces, than maintenance of this global network—at least for a while. The key reason is *not*, as some wrongly suggest, that having the forces overseas per se is necessarily a lot more expensive than basing them at home.[1] Especially in places where bases are well established on the territories of other modern nations, the incremental costs of having them outside American territory are typically at most a few percent of their total expense and often less. What is expensive is having a large military, regardless of where it is based. Operating abroad in austere environments like Iraq and Afghanistan is also costly.

But many of these costs may be worth paying. If we drew back, allies and interests might start to be threatened around the world, Iran might menace friends and oil interests in the Middle East, and China might find it more advantageous to push its growing weight around in East Asia.

Numerous friends and allies of the United States might then pursue larger armies and in some cases nuclear arsenals in response to unchecked dangers that they had to face alone. Previous periods in human history in which multiple states competed for influence and security without strong security alliances or structures to regulate and constrain the competition, such as Europe for most of the centuries leading up to the world wars, should give ample pause to those who believe that an international system without a strong central power could remain stable for long. The general absence of major interstate war that has, with very few exceptions, characterized most of post–World War II history would be put at serious risk.

Take a moment more to focus again on China. This enormously impressive yet challenging country requires a sophisticated American approach. It is neither really pure friend nor adversary. We are in both a partnership with China *and* a competitive relationship. We are not used to playing this role and so sometimes America's China policy seems to oscillate between hopes for sustained friendship, on the one hand, and occasional bouts of fear or anxiety on the other. Yet what we need is a policy that addresses *both* China's promise and its potential perils simultaneously. One can think of this as pursuing a positive relationship while hedging against the possibility that things go south.

But it may be even more useful, and accurate, to think of America's challenge as setting the conditions that maximize our odds of getting along well with China. That requires among other things a military policy that is not provocative or belligerent—but that is instead resolute and clear. Even during the Obama presidency, China has been trying to muscle its neighbors in the South China Sea area into accepting Chinese dominance of most of that international waterway, while also trying to pressure the United States not to operate its Navy in the Yellow Sea (also an international waterway) and getting tough with Japan over disputed territories in the East China Sea. Its goal seems not so much to prepare for open hostilities as to follow the dictums of the great ancient Chinese strategist Sun Tzu and win without fighting.[2] The United States has pushed back, operating its Navy where it chooses and organizing a coalition of countries to assert their rights to disputed maritime regions so that Beijing could not play divide and conquer. Backing it all up was the presence of American forces in the region. That capability reminded all parties that the United States is a Pacific power that will stand up for its friends in that region. Washington also thereby provides the glue needed so that the region's democracies (and some not-so-democratic states like Vietnam) can stand firmly together against any external threat if need be. This approach works.

We should not lightly discard it. It is with this philosophy in mind that we need to shape and structure our future East Asia/Pacific military deployments.

To play this global role, alone among the world's major powers the United States today has a substantial overseas military presence. It possesses enough capability in numerous strategically important parts of the world to make a difference in normal day-to-day regional balances of power, and to train vigorously with allies on a routine basis. Not only does the United States have a great deal of firepower stationed abroad, it has the infrastructure, the working relationships, and the transportation and logistics assets needed to reinforce its capacities quickly as needed in crises. This has been continuously true since World War II—so long that we now take it for granted. But stationing hundreds of thousands of troops abroad is not an automatic or inherent characteristic of major powers, especially in the modern postimperial era. No other major power has more than twenty thousand to thirty thousand forces abroad, with Britain and France leading the way after the United States. Substantial powers such as Russia, China, and India deploy forces totaling only in the thousands normally, as do several countries that participate frequently in peacekeeping missions.[3]

In some cases, foreign bases in the right place can actually save substantial sums of money. For example, being able to base U.S. tactical airpower at Kadena Air Base on Okinawa, Japan, arguably saves the United States several billion dollars a year. If the United States had to sustain a comparable airpower capability continuously in that region through other means, the alternative to Kadena might well be a larger Navy aircraft carrier fleet expanded by three or four carrier battle groups with an annual price tag of some $20 billion.[4]

As noted, American forces abroad are concentrated in three main zones—Europe, with close to 100,000 GIs; East Asia, with a comparably sized force; and the broader Middle East. In Europe, the largest presence by far is in Germany (around 50,000 troops currently). The United States also has almost 10,000 troops in the United Kingdom, mostly airmen and airwomen, and almost another 10,000 in Italy distributed relatively evenly among Air Force, Navy, and Army personnel. There are more than 1,000 U.S. troops per country in Spain, Belgium, and Turkey as well as more modest numbers elsewhere in Europe.[5]

In Northeast Asia, the largest presence is in Japan with about 35,000 American uniformed personnel, but U.S. capabilities in Korea with almost 30,000 GIs are not far behind. Even though they are obviously American soil, Hawaii, Alaska, and Guam are of course highly relevant to the Asia-Pacific region too—and they have about 40,000, 20,000, and 3,000 uniformed personnel on their territories, respectively.

Third is the Central Command region. Afghanistan is currently the dominant deployment of course, with close to 100,000 Americans in uniform there. Some 50,000 uniformed personnel are in the general Persian Gulf area, though those numbers continue to drop with the ending of the U.S. mission in Iraq. There are smaller but significant forces also in Egypt and Djibouti. Diego Garcia island, in the center of the Indian Ocean, is a very important base as well.[6]

In many regions abroad, American forces are present but distinguished by their small numbers. In Latin America, responses to disasters like the Haiti and Chile earthquakes of modern times typically involved only a few hundred troops, often National Guard men and women, for sustained periods.[7]

The Bush administration conducted a fairly thorough review of global basing known commonly as the Global Posture Review. It was intended to make sense of new strategic conditions brought about by 9/11, the rise of China, and other geostrategic changes. It was a positive legacy of an otherwise highly controversial secretary of defense,

Donald Rumsfeld, and has been largely sustained by the Obama administration.[8]

The Global Posture Review encompassed everything from the creation of new, generally modest bases in central Asia and eastern Europe to the further downsizing of the U.S. military presence in Germany to a reduction and realignment of the American presence in South Korea as well as Okinawa, Japan, along with increases in Guam. Of course, there have also been enormous changes in the Persian Gulf, related to the war in Iraq as well as the subsequent removal of American combat forces from Saudi Arabia and Turkey.

There is still a good deal of continuity with the past, though. Even with the implementation of the plan, the United States will retain some five hundred overseas sites with a combined value around $100 billion.[9] The budgetary costs of relocating forces, especially in Korea and Japan, could range up to $50 billion. Much of that would be associated with moving some seven thousand Marines from Okinawa to Guam—costs that would be likely borne in part by Tokyo, if it can sort out the Japanese domestic politics of getting the basic idea approved in the first place. Opposition on Okinawa to one aspect of the plan that would entail building a new airfield on a different part of the island may sink the whole concept.[10]

While big, the Rumsfeld review was hardly radical or unprecedented in scope. Less than twenty years ago, in the aftermath of the Cold War, much larger changes occurred in America's European base network, and 200,000 GIs came home as a result. The Vietnam and Korean wars had themselves produced much larger overall shifts in forces in previous decades. The British departure from the broader Middle East region in the 1960s and early 1970s, together with the Soviet invasion of Afghanistan, had led to momentous shifts in the American role in that region before as well. And of course, even all these changes pale in comparison with what happened in the 1940s and early 1950s, when America fully became a global power, then tried to come home after World War II, and then realized it could not do so when the Cold War began.

But the recent modifications have been significant nonetheless. Moreover, the Bush review was done with a broader approach than most previous base realignments, governed as they often were by the simple need to downsize after war or "upsize" for possible war against a specific foe such as the Soviet Union. By contrast, the latest review was guided by an effort to prepare for various possible scenarios—"planning for uncertainty" as the Rumsfeld Pentagon liked to say. It was nearly as notable for its decisions to increase certain forces and capabilities overseas as its decisions to cut others back.

Of course, global presence is not just about permanent facilities ashore. It also involves naval presence in key waterways. And it involves the ability to reinforce capabilities in the event of crisis or war.

The U.S. Navy these days is maintaining a robust global presence with only about 286 major warships. That is still a formidable force of generally high-technology and large vessels, to be sure, including 11 large-deck aircraft carriers, 11 large amphibious ships with aerial capability themselves, and more than 50 state-of-the-art nuclear-powered attack submarines.[11] But it is a fleet only half the size of its peak under Ronald Reagan. Yet it is maintaining 15 percent more overseas deployment time than it did a decade ago, just before 9/11. The Navy finds this an uncomfortably high tempo and wants to expand the fleet by about 10 percent, to 313 ships.[12] My own views, discussed further below, are that there are innovative ways to use the existing fleet or indeed a slightly smaller one to get the job done without such an expansion.

The United States has other assets that should be seen as part of its prompt global reach capabilities. Chief long-range strike assets feature the Air Force's 180 bombers—65

B-1, 20 B-2, and 94 B-52 aircraft. These, as well as transport planes, tactical aircraft, and support aircraft for purposes such as intelligence, make use of roughly 60 KC-10 tankers as well as nearly 200 KC-135 tanker aircraft (and more than 300 additional KC-135s in the Air Reserves and Air National Guard). These tankers, combined with America's dispersed base network, also allow tactical combat aircraft to be deployed quickly, assuming bases can be found for them in the region of operation. The United States Air Force has 1,700 such combat aircraft in its active-duty inventory alone, so depending on base access, this can be quite a potent capability (as the planes can of course deploy within days if they have somewhere to operate once reaching their destination).

Then there are prepositioned supplies in key overseas theaters that facilitate rapid reinforcement of additional combat capabilities if needed. They include huge ships stocked with enough weaponry and ammunition for several ground combat brigades in places like Guam and Diego Garcia, as well as ground-based facilities storing weaponry and supplies in places like Kuwait.

So where do we go from here in an age of austerity? In light of the above, what considerations should guide us as we seek to save money in our global basing and deployment practices?

As noted above, building new facilities is costly. Operating forces in austere environments like Afghanistan is very costly. And keeping forces in the military that would otherwise be unnecessary is expensive too. Any basing concepts that involve such choices have major budgetary implications.

That said, the year-to-year budgetary importance of overseas basing is not great in places where established facilities exist and allies help support them. In these cases, U.S. military salaries are not higher abroad; the cost of maintaining and operating facilities is not notably different; the price of weaponry operated by troops is generally the same; the civilian labor hired to work at the various defense installations is typically comparable as well. It is only more minor areas of expenditure where there could be some differences, for example in moving people around and providing them home leave in the United States, or providing American schools abroad. But these costs are modest—typically in the hundreds of millions of dollars a year for forces numbering in the tens of thousands range, for example.[13] Real savings thus come from bringing troops home from war theaters, or from not only shutting down bases abroad but eliminating the units that were previously stationed abroad from the force structure (and thereby making the net size of the U.S. military less than before).

On balance, the total costs to the American taxpayer of having U.S. forces abroad in Europe and East Asia total in the general range of around $3 billion a year. Perhaps $1 billion of that comes from the added expenses of moving people around and taking care of them with amenities like military schools. The other $2 billion comes from standing overseas military commands—which often exist for each individual service, as well as in the overall joint commands like European Command or U.S. Forces/Korea. There are at least a dozen such headquarters spread around Europe and East Asia, each typically manned by up to several hundred troops and comparable numbers of civilians. Factoring in their equipment, a $2 billion annual estimate is the right ballpark. However, the American combat forces that some-times are based on these foreign lands, being usable else-where in the world, are flexible enough that their costs should not be assigned directly to the defense of the coun-try in which they are located.[14]

The above considerations suggest that the main way we can save money from our current global patterns of deploy-ment, apart from ending the wars as effectively as possible, probably involves Navy capabilities rather than permanent bases on land. After an impressive decade or so of innova-tion largely in the 1990s, the Navy has slowed down some of its efforts to be more creative and reverted to a more classic approach of arguing for a larger fleet. But there may be other options.

Historically, the Navy has wished to sustain major deployments continuously in the Mediterranean, Persian Gulf area, and western Pacific. Since the Cold War ended, the Mediterranean has been deemphasized to a degree, but the Persian Gulf area has received even more attention than before, with no sign of that abating despite the overthrow of Saddam and the departure of most U.S. forces from Iraq. On balance, as noted above, naval requirements have not diminished in recent years, yet the size of the fleet has.

In the first decade after the Cold War, seeing the writing on the wall, the Navy got more innovative. It based some specialty ships like minesweepers overseas, rotating crews by airplane to allow sailors a break without having to waste time bringing the ships home. It also chose to tolerate gaps in naval presence in some theaters, viewing predictability and consistency as less important than before, and "surging" forces at unpredictable times and places instead. Where some degree of steady presence was viewed as necessary, the Navy would sometimes provide that capability with smaller surface ships or large-deck amphibious vessels rather than aircraft carriers as well. All of this made sense.[15]

However, the Navy appears to have stalled a bit in its innovations. While crews are rotated with minesweepers, a handful of coastal patrol craft, and (as has long been the case) the ballistic missile submarine force, the practice has not been extended to other ships. Successful experiments have been done with larger vessels, but the Navy has not chosen to adopt the crew-rotation practice. This means that a typical surface combatant, like a cruiser or destroyer, spends about six months in home port training up for a deployment, then sails for a six-month mission abroad but consumes perhaps two of those months in transit, and then spends another period of at least six months back in home port for recovery and maintenance and other such activities. The net effect is four months on station out of every eighteen- to twenty-four-month period, a very inefficient cycle.

There is a better way. By keeping a given ship abroad for a couple years and having two crews share that vessel overseas as well as a training ship at home, the Navy can do more with less. In fact, it can improve its deployment efficiency by up to 40 percent per ship, accomplishing with about 3.5 ships, on average, what previously might have required 5. Focusing on the Navy's large surface combatants, cruisers and destroyers, this approach could allow roughly 54 ships to maintain the global presence that the Navy says it needs (of about 21 of these ships deployed abroad at a time) rather than the target of 88 ships it currently is pursuing.[16]

This logic should not be pushed to extremes. Not all of the Navy's ships can be rotated the same way. It is very difficult to imagine applying this concept to aircraft carriers, with their combined crews of up to five thousand (in contrast to more like three hundred sailors on major surface combatants). For carriers, the main alternative to current practice is probably to focus somewhat less on the Mediterranean in normal times, and to use large-deck amphibious ships (with their short-takeoff, vertical landing planes and helicopters) rather than carriers for some routine missions.

This new system of crew rotation would have certain modest additional costs (e.g., flying crews around the world) but it would also yield operating savings by reducing wasted steaming time crossing oceans. It would take time to implement, however. New practices would have to be worked out, and access to overseas port facilities expanded for routine sustenance and maintenance functions. The Navy is already seeing higher maintenance deficits, due to strain on equipment, and cannot implement such a new approach to presence until it has facilities abroad that can keep its fleet shipshape.[17]

One more reason for caution: the Navy cannot lose sight of new operating regions, such as the increasingly ice-free and thus navigable Arctic. One need not imagine a new "cold" war in the far north to be aware that the defense of basic Western interests requires some degree of occasional American and allied presence.[18]

Any new plan for how the Navy can size, and operate, its fleet also needs to bear in mind possible warfighting requirements. Among other things, the Navy needs extra ships as an attrition reserve should some vessels be sunk in future conflict. This is discussed further in chapter 8, where I "stress test" the new recommended force posture against the Iranian and Chinese challenges. Thus, Navy force structure should not be reduced by the full amount that a simple and comprehensive arithmetic application of this crew-rotation concept might theoretically allow—with reductions of dozens of ships.[19] A reduction of about twenty surface combatants would be a more reasonable and prudent change.

An additional way to get more out of a smaller fleet is to homeport more ships near the theaters where they operate. That helps reduce time wasted in transit. Indeed, about a decade ago, the Navy started down this path in another important way, basing three attack submarines on Guam.[20] But the Navy can go well beyond the idea of stationing three submarines there; in fact there is room to add at least eight more. The average number of mission days for a submarine stationed so near the western Pacific theater might be about one hundred a year, roughly three times what a submarine stationed in the continental United States can muster. Adding six more submarines to Guam would allow a reduction of up to ten attack submarines in the overall force structure and save an annual average of roughly $1 billion without a reduction in mission effectiveness.[21]

Forward homeporting need not be limited to the attack submarine fleet. Even with the Navy's new approach to flexible deployments, homeporting a second carrier closer to a key theater of operations makes good sense. The idea of moving a carrier from California to either Hawaii or Guam merits serious attention.[22] By previous patterns of carrier deployments, homeports in California necessitated travels of some two weeks to East Asia and three or more weeks to the Persian Gulf.[23] Homeporting in Hawaii or Guam can shave five to ten days off that time, each way.

A carrier based farther west in the Pacific may prove somewhat more vulnerable tactically than one based back home—good reason not to extend this idea to several carriers. But on the other side of things, stationing multiple carriers in a single port *anywhere* creates the possibility of a single point of failure or vulnerability. So taking an aircraft carrier out of a port like San Diego where several are normally present, and instead stationing it in Hawaii or Guam where we presently have none, makes logical sense from a force protection standpoint as well. Although it seems unlikely to be possible given political constraints in Japan,

Global Distribution of Military Spending, 2009
Millions of current dollars

Country	Defense expenditure	Precentage of Global total	Cumulative percentage
United States	661,049	45.3%	45%
Formal U.S. Allies			
NATO			
Canada	19,575	1.3%	47%
France	54,446	3.7%	50%
Germany	47,466	3.3%	54%
Italy	30,489	2.1%	56%
Spain	16,944	1.2%	57%
Turkey	10,883	0.7%	58%
United Kingdom	59,131	4.1%	62%
Rest of NATO (1)	61,848	4.2%	66%
Total NATO (excluding U.S.)	300,782		
Total NATO	961,831		
Rio Pact (2)	48,530	3.3%	69%
Key Asia-Pacific Allies			
Japan	51,085	3.5%	73%
South Korea	22,439	1.5%	74%
Australia	19,515	1.3%	76%
New Zealand	1,358	0.1%	76%
Thailand	4,732	0.3%	76%
Philippines	1,363	0.1%	76%
Total Key Asia-Pacific Allies	100,492		
Informal U.S. Allies			
Israel	13,516	0.9%	77%
Egypt	4,118	0.3%	77%
Iraq	4,118	0.3%	78%
Pakistan	3,811	0.3%	78%
Gulf Cooperation Council (3)	59,720	4.1%	82%
Jordan	1,393	0.1%	82%
Morocco	3,061	0.2%	82%
Mexico	4,796	0.3%	83%
Taiwan	9,500	0.7%	83%
Total Informal Allies	104,033		
Other Nations			
Non-NATO Europe	24,258	1.7%	85%
Other Middle East and North Africa (4)	9,945	0.7%	86%
Other Central and South Asia (5)	4,435	0.3%	86%
Other East Asia and Pacific (6)	14,606	1.0%	87%
Other Caribbean and Latin America (7)	141	0.0%	87%
Sub-Saharan Africa	15,146	1.0%	88%
Total Other Nations	68,531		
Major Neutral Nations			
China (8)	70,381	4.8%	93%
Russia	38,293	2.6%	95%
India	38,278	2.6%	98%
Indonesia	4,821	0.3%	98%
Total Major Neutral Nations	151,733		

Country	Defense expenditure	Precentage of Global total	Cumulative percentage
Nemeses and Adversaries			
Iran	8,636	0.6%	99%
North Korea (9)	5,000	0.3%	99%
Syria	2,229	0.2%	99%
Myanmar	2,000	0.1%	100%
Venezuela	3,316	0.2%	100%
Cuba	1,960	0.1%	100%
Total Nemeses and Adversaries	23,141		
TOTAL	1,459,283	100%	

Source: International Institute for Strategic Studies, *The Military Balance 2011* (New York: Routledge Press, 2011), pp. 471-477

1 - Albania, Belgium, Bulgaria, Croatia, Czech Republic, Denmark, Estonia, Greece, Hungary, Iceland, Latvia, Lithuania, Luxembourg, Netherlands, Norway, Poland, Portugal, Romania, Slovakia, and Slovenia.
2 - Argentina, Bahamas, Bolivia, Brazil, Chile, Colombia, Costa Rica, Dominican Republic, Ecuador, El Salvador, Guatemala, Haiti, Honduras, Nicaragua, Panama, Paraguay, Peru, Trinidad and Tobago, and Uruguay.
3 - Bahrain, Kuwait, Oman, Qatar, Saudi Arabia, United Arab Emirates.
4 - Algeria, Lebanon, Libya, Mauritania, Tunisia, and Yemen.
5 - Afghanistan, Bangladesh, Kazakhstan, Kyrgyzstan, Maldives, Nepal, Sri Lanka, Tajikistan, Turkmenistan, and Uzbekistan.
6 - Brunei, Cambodia, Fiji, Laos, Malaysia, Mongolia, Papua New Guinea, Singapore, Timor Leste, and Vietnam.
7 - Antigua and Barbuda, Barbados, Belize, Jamaica, and Suriname.
8 - The U.S. government estimate is more than twice the amount shown, equaling roughly 10% of the global total.
9 - North Korea and Myanmar are author estimates. Figures were added to overall total.

there is even an argument for homeporting a second carrier there, whether in Yokosuka or somewhere else.[24] Even with such a change, though, the Navy will need ample carriers for sustained crisis response in a place like the waters near Taiwan, as discussed further in chapter 8—again, placing a floor below which force structure cuts should not descend.

On balance, the Navy does not need to add 10 percent more vessels to its force structure to carry out current practices and presence. Indeed, it can do well with 10 percent less, or about 250 major ships.

One part of the current U.S. plan for relocating facilities abroad does need rethinking—the previously mentioned idea of relocating several thousand Marines from Okinawa to Guam while also relocating a key Marine Corps airfield known as Futenma to a more northern area on Okinawa as an offshore facility. In addition to the political problems it has created in Japan, this plan would cost the United States more than $15 billion. It is a dubious proposition. Instead, many of these Marines can be brought back to bases in the United States (where space will be available as the Marine Corps gets smaller in the years ahead). To shore up allied capabilities and make it clear that we are not weakening our combined commitment to East Asian security, Japan and the United States could take several compensating measures, such as purchasing at least one regiment's worth of equipment and a prepositioning ship to store it on, and basing that ship permanently in Japanese waters. Marines from California or Hawaii could then fly in to meet that equipment in the event of a crisis, marrying up with it in Japan or perhaps somewhere else in the region. That capability, plus more rigorous allied planning to allow Marines also to redeploy to Okinawa in a crisis (using Japanese military and civilian facilities as well as U.S. bases), would signal resolve and maintain rapid-reaction capability at lower cost. Meanwhile, a smaller Futenma replacement airfield might be built within one of the larger existing American bases in northern Okinawa.

CHAPTER SEVEN

Equipping and Modernizing the Force

Until this point the book has focused mostly on people, units, and formations. But what about weaponry and other equipment? Surely that must be where lots of the money is, given Eisenhower's earlier warnings about a military-industrial complex and all the stories that continue to pop up in the press about weapons costs growing out of control in so many instances? Surely we can save money here too.

Just think of what we have added to the U.S. military arsenal in modern times, even after the great military revolutions that arrived before and during World War II. The 1950s brought helicopters and ICBMs and jets. The 1960s and 1970s brought satellites and night-vision technology. The 1980s and 1990s gave us stealth airplanes and precision strike weapons in abundance. The last ten years have seen the coming of age of drones and other robotics, as well as lightning-fast communications systems that tie warfighters together in real time on the battlefield. And that is just a partial list. Is it time to slow down our military modernization efforts? Are there places we can save money? Does defense modernization now occur almost by autopilot, due to an overly influential military-industrial complex of the type Eisenhower warned against, whether we need everything we buy or not?

It is true that we can rethink a number of weapons efforts. Some weapons are bought partly out of bureaucratic inertia as well as logrolling of the Congress. But the above list of new capabilities should also remind us of the benefits of innovation—and yes, the strengths and accomplishments of that much-derided American military-industrial complex. Often vilified in peacetime as profit seekers, U.S. defense firms (and their foreign counterparts at times) consistently equip America's men and women in arms with the finest military equipment in the world when they go into combat.

There is big money involved and some of it can be reduced. The so-called acquisition accounts—primarily research, development, testing, and evaluation, or RDT&E, on the one hand, and procurement on the other—together cost the nation almost $200 billion a year in the core defense budget. This is more, by far, than any other country on Earth spends on its entire military establishment, and probably five times more than China spends on hardware today itself. It is also true that, just in major weapons systems alone, the Pentagon has close to a trillion dollars of plans on the books for the years ahead, completing development and production of weapons it already has in the pipeline.

Yet these acquisition costs do not constitute the preponderance of the Department of Defense's budget. They represent about 35 percent of the $550 billion or so in core defense spending. As such, we have to avoid the common mistake of thinking that the best way to cut the defense budget is always to cut acquisition programs.[1]

Moreover, for all the stories of expensive weapons, the flip side of the reality is that American military technology generally performs extremely well in combat. Examples include Operation Desert Storm, the overthrow of the Taliban in Afghanistan in 2001, the rapid invasion of Iraq and Thunder Run through Baghdad in 2003, the rapid deployment and sustained support of U.S. forces in the field during all these and other operations, the magnificent intelligence and command and control networks that facilitate rapid targeting of extremists on the battlefield and around the world, and the development of drone technology to complement earlier breakthroughs in areas like stealth and precision mu-

Age of Active Duty Aircraft Fleet for U.S. Air Force
(as of September 30, 2010)

Type	Age in Years									Total	Average
	0-3	3-6	6-9	9-12	12-15	15-18	18-21	21-24	24+		
A-10									184	184	28.6
B-1								65		65	23.1
B-2					7	9	3	1		20	16.1
B-52									65	65	48.8
C-5								29	7	36	24.3
(K)C-10							1	11	47	59	25.7
C-12	30	1	4	2		19	4	4		64	14.4
C-17	37	35	42	31	19				23	187	8.1
C-20						1	1	9		11	21.7
C-21									35	35	25.7
(V)C-25							2			2	19.9
C-32				2	2					4	12.0
C-37	2		3	6						11	8.2
C-40		2	2							4	6.6
C-130	28	10	1	4		15	20	22	159	259	30.1
C-135									213	213	48.6
CV-22	9	7								16	2.6
E-3									31	31	30.8
E-4									4	4	36.6
E-9A									2	2	35.5

										Total	Percent
F-15C-D								1	26	87	114	26.5
F-15E		1							48		213	18.4
F-16		72	10	16	18	35	104	82	34	583	18.9
F-22	64		13	14		149	272			158	3.6
F-35	4		21	1						4	1.1
H-1									92	92	38.8
H-60				5	1	5	37	10	10	68	20.4
MQ-1	69	69								138	TK
MQ-9	38	9	1							48	1.7
RQ-4	14	9	2							25	3.0
T-1					57	99	21			177	15.9
T-6	94	130	87	34						345	4.9
T-38									434	434	43.2
T-41									4	4	41.1
T-43									3	3	36.3
T-51		3								3	5.1
U-2						1	1	8	23	32	27.2
UV-18					1				2	3	26.5
Gliders			30							31	8.7
Total	**389**	**348**	**216**	**115**	**105**	**333**	**467**	**315**	**1459**	**3747**	**23.0**
Percent	10.4%	9.3%	5.8%	3.1%	2.8%	8.9%	12.5%	8.4%	38.9%		

Source: "2011 USAF Almanac," Air Force (May 2011), p. 52
http://www.airforce-magazine.com/MagazineArchive/Magazine%20Documents/2011/May%202011/0511facts_figs.pdf

Department of Defense Annual Budget Authority for Procurement and Research Development Test & Evaluation (RDT&E), FY 1948–2016
Billions of 2011 dollars

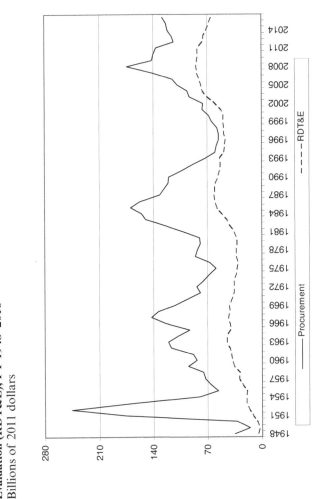

Source: U.S. Department of Defense, *National Defense Budget Estimates for FY 2012* (Washington, March 2011), pp. 123–128.

Figures are based on the president's budget request for 2012. Totals prior to 2012 include all enacted war and supplemental funding. Figures for 2012 and beyond do not include estimates of nitions. These are striking testaments to scientific and industrial excellence on the part of America's laboratories, weapons development teams, and manufacturers.

Cutting modernization plans for the U.S. military was the core of the approach to reducing defense spending in the 1990s, when annual procurement budgets were reduced by two thirds relative to earlier Reagan-era highs. But that was an unusual historical moment. The United States could take a "procurement holiday" of sorts since it had recently bought so much new equipment during that Reagan buildup, and since the concomitant reduction of the combat force structure allowed older equipment to be selectively retired first. We could afford not to buy much in the 1990s because we had purchased so much in the 1980s. There is no large inventory of new equipment today that can allow us such a budgetary reprieve in the coming decade. In particular, much of that Reagan-era equipment is still around, but now in need of replacement—not just to modernize the force, but simply to keep it safe and reliable.

The 1990s cutbacks were not easy on industry or the economy, of course. Softening the pain to an extent, however, was the fact that the 1980s had been a fairly good decade for the defense business. In addition, even though the economy was mediocre in the early part of the 1990s in the United States—and even though defense cutbacks exacerbated the difficulty in some cases[2]—the situation rapidly improved. As the 1990s progressed, the general health of the U.S. economy strengthened, creating new jobs in other sectors.

The situation is different today. The national economy is much weaker. The defense sector is also smaller. The number of workers in aerospace and defense is down from more than 1 million in 1991 to just over 600,000 two decades later, exemplifying the tendency of the U.S. manufacturing base writ large to lose lots of jobs over that period.[3] In addition, there are now just five major contractors in the defense business—Boeing, Raytheon, Northrop Grumman, Lockheed Martin, and General Dynamics. Often the number capable of creating a given type of weapon system is just one or two. As such, the health of the industrial base needs to be kept in mind, since budgets are not so large as to guarantee a diverse and strong national security industrial base absent considerable care and attentiveness.[4] Certain capabilities could simply be lost, and take years to re-create.[5] The ability to keep costs in check through competition can also be lost.[6]

In addition, even though current acquisition budgets are sizable in real-dollar terms, the growing cost of weaponry means that these budgets typically fund far fewer major programs than was the case before. That reality is reinforced by the fact that more of today's acquisition budget is devoted to research and development rather than production—

perhaps a reasonable approach at a time of rapid technology change, but still a tendency that deprives procurement accounts of the share of funds they used to receive.

All that said, not all weapons are equally necessary. And we cannot cut the defense budget by a large amount while sparing weapons accounts. Not counting war costs, the Pentagon's procurement budget exceeds $100 billion a year. Its RDT&E budget adds another $80 billion, the latter figure in particular being quite robust by historical standards.[7] Completing big-ticket programs that are now under way will cost an estimated $850 billion from 2012 through completion of their various acquisition schedules. (Roughly an equal amount has already been spent cumulatively on those same programs, meaning the total cost for acquisition will cumulatively be $1.7 trillion over the lifetime of the programs.) So there is clearly a lot of money to consider.[8]

A few caveats and constraints about the possibility of reaping easy savings from weapons cutbacks should be kept in mind, however. First, despite the claims of some defense budget cutters, few if any of these systems can today be described as "Cold War legacy weapons." That common refrain makes it sound as if the Pentagon has simply retained weapons it should have eliminated twenty years ago out of inertia. While inertia, and bureaucratic as well as parochial politics, can play a role in the defense budgeting process, there is no weapon today being justified on the grounds that it might be needed against a Soviet-like threat. Rather, worries that adversaries could employ advanced surface-to-air, air-to-air, antiship, and ground attack missiles, quiet diesel submarines, sophisticated mines, and other such assets including stealthy planes of their own drive the Pentagon's desires for stealth, speed, maneuverability, and related characteristics in future weaponry.

Second, while it may be tempting to cut weapons that experience cost overruns, it is also natural to expect some state-of-the-art weapons to cost more than originally foreseen since they involve new ideas and technologies. That said, things have gotten a bit out of hand of late with cost overruns. By 2008, the top defense programs together had cumulative cost overruns of nearly $300 billion (the comparable figure had been $43 billion in 2000). Secretary Gates made some headway against this challenge with his weapons cancellations, and more is needed, as long as we bear in mind that *some* cost growth is a normal characteristic of the process of invention.[9]

Third, if a weapons procurement plan is scaled back in numbers, unit costs usually go up by at least 10 percent and sometimes more. For example, cutting a production run by two thirds might increase costs 15 percent to 50 percent, roughly speaking, depending on a range of factors.[10] Fourth, unless the combat units that were to receive the new weaponry are simply eliminated, the cancellation of the weaponry would not in fact change the need to buy *something* serviceable and safe and reliable to equip those units. As a rule, weapons costing at least half as much as the canceled systems will be needed.[11] And with today's Air Force tactical aircraft averaging more than twenty years in age, as well as Navy and Marine Corps aircraft averaging more than fifteen, purchasing some types of new planes—not to mention other types of systems in similar straits—cannot be deferred.[12]

And finally, it is clearly possible to push thinking about economizing too far. A number of thoughtful analysts have already lamented the declining size of the U.S. Navy, for example, at a time when China is being more assertive in seas around its borders and when Iran continues to pose a major threat to the broader Persian Gulf. Analysts have also expressed concern about too much emphasis on America's current wars at the budgetary expense of other possible missions and scenarios. They worry for example about the nation's relatively low investments in long-range strike platforms (like a new bomber or a longer-range unmanned aerial vehicle flown from an aircraft carrier) at a time when China is becoming more powerful *and* when technologies that can attack ports and airfields in forward theaters are becoming more prevalent.[13]

Selected Acquisition Report Program Acquisition Cost Summary
(as of December 31, 2010)

Weapons system	Base year	Base year dollars	Current dollars	Quantity
Army				
AB3A REMANUFACTURE	2010	7,064.40	8,093.90	602
AB3B NEV	2010	2,307.00	2,510.40	56
ATIRCM/CMWS - ATIRCM	2003	894.8	1,054.40	-
ATIRCM/CMWS - CMWS	2003	1,900.90	2,186.20	2,668
CH-47F	2005	10,614.80	12,147.40	512
EXCALIBUR	2007	2,264.60	2,518.70	30,388
FBCB2	2005	1,579.90	1,556.70	22,248
FMTV	1996	11,594.20	18,921.30	85,488
GMLRS/GMLRS AW	2003	9,780.20	11,848.90	140,239
HIMARS	2003	3,711.60	4,388.40	894
IAMD	2009	4,856.60	5,791.60	296
INCREMENT 1 E-IBCT	2010	3,149.50	3,284.00	9
JLENS	2005	5,850.00	7,151.00	16
LONGBOW APACHE	1996	5,690.60	7,027.80	758
LUH	2006	1,638.30	1,883.00	322
MQ-1C UAS GRAY EAGLE	2010	4,923.60	5,220.80	13
PATRIOT PAC-3	2002	9,084.00	9,205.80	1,159
PATRIOT/MEADS CAP -FIRE UNIT	2004	16,530.50	21,839.40	48
PATRIOT/MEADS CAP -MISSILE	2004	6,220.90	8,056.00	1,528
STRYKER	2004	8,276.90	8,534.70	2,096
UH-60M BLACK HAWK	2005	16,801.70	20,847.10	1,235
WIN-T INCREMENT 1	2007	3,798.00	3,879.70	1,677
WIN-T INCREMENT 2	2010	4,686.00	4,996.90	2,216
WIN-T INCREMENT 3	2009	15,807.90	18,813.20	3,428
Subtotal, Army		159,026.90	191,757.30	
Navy				
AGM-88E AARGM	2003	1,528.50	1,861.40	1,919
AIM-9X	1997	2,464.00	3,232.90	10,049
CEC	2002	4,123.30	4,310.70	272
CH-53K	2006	14,980.90	18,766.30	156
COBRA JUDY REPLACEMENT	2003	1,365.00	1,464.00	1
CVN 78 CLASS	2000	28,701.20	36,082.10	3
DDG 1000	2005	31,547.90	36,296.30	10
DDG 51	1987	16,953.70	20,117.50	23
E-2D AHE	2009	17,468.60	19,031.40	75
EA-18G	2004	7,530.80	8,636.40	84
EFV	2007	8,493.20	8,725.20	1,025
F/A-18E/F	2000	38,884.70	41,637.30	458
H-1 UPGRADES (4BW/4BN)	2008	11,203.40	12,186.80	353
IDECM - IDECM Blocks 2/3	2008	1,410.90	1,535.20	12,809
IDECM - IDECM Block 4	2008	660.7	746.1	160
JHSV	2008	3,460.00	3,892.30	18
JOINT MRAP	2008	22,013.50	22,415.00	15,374
JPALS	2008	963.2	1,031.90	37
JSOW (BASELINE/UNITARY) - BASELINE/BLU-108	1990	3,566.30	4,898.70	16,124
JSOW (BASELINE/UNITARY) - UNITARY	1990	1,977.80	2,974.80	7,000
LCS*	2010	28,570.90	33,837.60	2
LHA 6 AMERICA CLASS	2006	2,877.40	3,093.50	1
LPD 17	1996	9,018.10	10,761.80	12
MH-60R	2006	10,627.00	11,424.70	254
MH-60S	1998	5,270.10	6,093.80	237
MQ-4C UAS BAMS	2008	12,224.50	15,172.30	70
MUOS	2004	5,768.90	6,810.60	6
NMT	2002	1,923.40	2,321.10	333
P-8A	2010	30,271.90	31,428.60	115
RMS	2006	1,304.60	1,399.40	108
SM-6	2004	5,281.10	6,597.20	1,200
SSN 774	1995	64,353.60	93,207.30	30
TACTICAL TOMAHAWK	1999	2,977.30	3,290.30	2,790
T-AKE	2000	4,262.60	4,890.20	12
TRIDENT II MISSILE	1983	26,556.30	35,518.50	845
V-22	2005	50,250.40	53,253.40	458
VTUAV	2006	2,366.40	2,787.10	177
Subtotal, Navy		483,202.10	571,729.70	
Air Force				
AEHF	2002	5,800.70	6,085.70	3
AMRAAM	1992	12,278.20	13,112.40	15,450
ASIP	2010	539.6	508	4
B-2 EHF SATCOM AND COMPUTER INCREMENT 1	2007	659.7	706.1	21
B-2 RMP	2008	1,324.50	1,348.40	20
C-130 AMP	2010	5,930.20	6,300.30	221

C-130J	1996	730.7	839.7	11
C-27J	2007	3,635.20	4,087.80	78
C-5 AMP	2006	888.4	856.3	61
C-5 RERP	2008	7,146.60	7,694.10	52
F-22	2005	64,281.70	61,323.70	181
FAB-T	2002	2,642.30	3,167.40	216
GBS	1997	451.4	497.1	346
GPS IIIA	2010	3,840.80	4,002.30	8
HC/MC-130 RECAPITALIZATION	2009	8,078.10	8,745.30	74
JASSM Baseline	2010	2,890.50	2,679.70	2,947
JASSM -ER	2010	2,195.00	2,301.40	2,500
JDAM	1995	2,300.30	2,606.70	89,065
JPATS	2002	4,529.00	5,041.10	783
LAIRCM	2008	383.6	366	8
MP-RTIP	2000	1,449.30	1,568.40	-
MQ-9 UAS REAPER	2008	10,751.30	11,834.80	391
NAS	2005	1,373.20	1,421.10	93
NAVSTAR GPS - SPACE & CONTROL	2000	5,015.60	5,120.90	33
NAVSTAR GPS - USER EQUIPMENT	2000	797.8	874.40	-
NPOESS	2002	5,538.00	6,117.60	6
RQ-4A/B UAS GLOBAL HAWK	2000	4,350.30	5,394.00	63
SBIRS HIGH	1995	3,679.50	4,147.30	5
SBSS BLOCK 10	2007	810.5	825.8	1
SDB II	2010	4,577.50	5,210.40	17,163
WGS	2010	1,162.20	1,042.50	3
Subtotal, Air Force		170,031.70	175,826.70	
DoD				
AMF JTRS	2008	7,758.60	9,034.30	27,102
BMDS**	2002	95,322.70	111,899.10	-
CHEM DEMIL-ACWA	1994	1,957.40	2,430.40	-
CHEM DEMIL-CMA	1994	11,513.70	12,879.90	29,060
F-35	2002	177,100.00	233,000.00	2,866
JTRS GMR	2002	14,437.20	19,112.90	108,388
JTRS HMS	2004	8,569.00	10,717.00	328,674
JTRS NED	2002	812.9	914.4	-
MIDS	2003	1,824.80	1,818.90	2,964
Subtotal, DoD		319,296.30	401,806.90	

Source: U.S. Department of Defense, "Selected Acquisition Report (SAR) Summary Tables", December 2010
(http://www.acq.osd.mil/ara/am/sar/31Dec10Tables.pdf)

Totals may not add up because of rounding. Each weapon system is assigned a base year based on key milestones in its development; costs as expressed in "base year dollars" are measured in that base year's constant dollars. All procurement as well as research, development, test and evaluation are included. Actual costs can grow even more.

Savings are nonetheless quite possible. Today's military may not buy Cold War legacy systems as critics allege, but it does arguably overinsure. A case in point is air combat. Even as drones have become much more effective, even as precision-guided ordnance has become devastatingly accurate, even as real-time surveillance and information grids have evolved rapidly, plans for modernizing manned combat systems have remained essentially at previous levels.

Between them, for example, the Air Force, Navy, and Marine Corps still plan to buy 2,500 F-35 combat jets at a total acquisition price of more than $300 billion in constant 2011 dollars. Production is just beginning at low rates, with the big ramp-up expected in the next few years. The Pentagon will spend about $15 billion annually on the plane starting in mid-decade. Three fourths of the funds are yet to be spent. The Pentagon's independent cost assessment office believes the average unit procurement price could be 15 to 20 percent higher than official estimates, exceeding $110 million per plane in 2011 dollars. And once purchased, the same office estimates that the F-35 will also cost a third more to operate than planes like the F-16 and F-18 that it is replacing.[14]

Finding a logical alternative to the existing program is more complex than some allow. For example, some have criticized the Marine Corps variant of the plane, with its extra engine as needed for vertical landing. But in fact, that variant is important for an era in which airfields are increasingly vulnerable to precision ordnance of the types that countries such as Iran and China are fielding. The United States needs enough F-35Bs, as the Marine variant is known, to be able to populate bases nearest potential combat zones, such as the Gulf states (for scenarios involving Iran) and Okinawa (in regard to China). As Marine Corps commandant General James Amos has noted, there are ten times as many 3,000-foot runways in the world adequate for such short-takeoff jets as there are 8,000-foot runways suitable for conventional aircraft—and the Marines can also lay down an expeditionary 3,000-foot runway in a matter of days in other places.[15] We also need to plan on perhaps losing more aircraft in future combat, even with these added survivability features, than the numbers to which we have become accustomed in modern times.

In addition, either the F-35 aircraft will have to be bought, existing planes will have to be refurbished, or the size of tactical fighter forces will have to be reduced. There is no other option, because existing planes like the F-16, F-18, and Harrier jet are aging.[16] And if we are to buy the F-35 (or "Lightning II") in significant numbers, as we should given its stealthy features, it is important to get production lines running at efficient rates so that the unit cost of the plane becomes reasonable. The plane is now surmounting many of the development challenges it had previously encountered and is probably nearing the point where large-scale production makes sense.[17]

My alternative concept for the F-35 would then go something like this. Buy a total of 1,250 instead of 2,500. Leave the Marine Corps plan largely as is, scaling back only by 10 to 20 percent to account more fully for the proven capacity of unmanned aerial vehicles to carry out some missions previously handled by manned aircraft. Cancel the Navy variant, with its relatively limited range compared with likely needs—buying more F/A-18E/F Super Hornets in the meantime while committing more firmly to development of a longer-range unmanned carrier-capable attack aircraft.[18] Scale back Air Force numbers, currently expected to exceed 1,700 F-35 planes, by almost half.

Of the 800 planes that the Air Force was counting on, but will not get under this approach, make up the difference in the following ways. First, cut back the need by 200 planes by eliminating two tactical fighter wings as discussed before. Second, "take credit" for the 200 large combat-capable unmanned aerial vehicles (UAVs) currently owned by the Air Force, with at least 300 more on the way, and view them as viable replacements for manned fighter planes. These Predator and Reaper planes may not be one-for-one substitutes for fighters but they count for something (and the former cost $30 million apiece in contrast to more than $100 million for F-35s). The Air Force is buying the equivalent of five wings of large UAVs; perhaps it could eliminate two more manned fighter wings as a result.[19] For the remaining planes, employ some combination of new purchases of F-16 jets and refurbishments of existing F-16s to make up the difference as needed. This would ensure that pilots fly reliable, safe airframes but without the cost of buying state-of-the art equipment for the entire tactical combat aircraft inventory. This approach will save some $60 billion, net, in F-35 purchase costs. The F-16 option is still available since the production line is currently making aircraft for Morocco and Oman, but it may not remain open for more than a couple years, so this option would have to be exercised fairly promptly to make economic sense.[20] Additional savings in the Marine Corps and Navy will add up to another $20 billion to $25 billion.

Annual acquisition savings might be $5 billion—real money, to be sure, but also an example that reveals the difficulty of taking huge programs and responsibly translating them into less expensive alternatives. Over time up to another $2 billion a year or so in savings would be achievable in operating accounts from the sum total of all these changes in tactical aircraft (including the reduction in force structure). These savings will not kick in right away, since as noted it is important to get the F-35 production line working efficiently to keep unit costs in check.

It should also be remembered that a fair amount of risk is inherent in this alternative plan, since entirely canceling the F-35C Navy version of the plane will leave the Navy with aircraft that are less stealthy over the next decade. This is a risk, and probably a tolerable one, but not a trivial one. Again, cutting defense by up to 10 percent is hard, and going much beyond that is ill advised.

Following the logic of the discussion on aircraft, I would propose evaluating existing weapons modernization plans with an eye toward streamlining or canceling several of them according to the following criteria:

• Weapons making maximum use of the computer and communications revolutions should be considered highest priority. These offer arguably the greatest benefit for the most reasonable price tag—the best bang for the buck. Current trends in precision munitions, in computer technology, and in related fields such as robotics offer tremendous opportunities.[21]

• Weapons programs should, where possible, set realistic timelines and budget paths and quantity goals, and stick to them—advice that seems obvious but that is often not heeded.[22]

• Weapons that appear redundant should be least protected. Sometimes, bureaucratic inertia combined with America's great resource base allow its military to avoid tough choices.[23]

• Weapons that perform poorly, technically or financially, should of course be reassessed.[24]

• Weapons designed for less important missions, if these can be convincingly identified, should also receive lower priority. Nuclear weapons modernization and perhaps Marine Corps amphibious assault are possible examples here. One needs to be careful, though; sweeping conclusions about which types of warfare or scenarios are supposedly obsolete and which are the waves of the future prove wrong at least as often as they prove correct.[25]

In this light, changes to several areas of defense modernization beyond the F-35 example discussed above should be seriously considered (there are also procurement savings implied in chapter 5's discussion of a smaller Army and Marine Corps—but those savings will not be noted here to avoid double counting):[26]

1. Reduce spending on nuclear weapons. Ironically, one of the first acts of Congress after the Tea Party dominated the fall 2010 elections was to increase spending on the very kinds of weapons we are least likely ever to use, and most likely to be overdeploying today. This is of course the broad area of nuclear weapons. In December 2010, the issue was that conservative critics of the New START Treaty between the United States and Russia, concerned over the state of some of America's nuclear infrastructure, decided to withhold votes on treaty ratification until the administration promised to pledge more spending on nuclear weapons–related capabilities. There was a reasonable logic in this up to a point; the nation needs a reliable and safe nuclear arse-

nal and a modern nuclear infrastructure. As such, there is a case for building a simpler, safer, more reliable warhead without testing in the years ahead, among other measures.[27] But the problem is that we do not need all of the more than 1,500 strategic warheads allowed by the treaty, plus several thousand additional tactical and surplus warheads that are entirely unconstrained by this or any other international agreement. Nor do we need to hedge against a revanchist Russia by retaining the capability to rapidly upload nuclear forces on missiles so that they can carry even more weapons in the future. Our bomber fleet, most of which is now focused on conventional military missions, provides ample insurance against Russian cheating. If Russia did cheat, we would in fact need some kind of response, but the situation would still be far less foreboding than in the Cold War.

This change in philosophy would keep us at nuclear parity with Russia—a country over which we now have enormous conventional military dominance, providing further reassurance. And it would save money—in the missile forces of the Department of Defense and in the nuclear-related activities of the Department of Energy. Termination of the "D5" SLBM (submarine-launched ballistic missile) nuclear-tipped missile program would be possible. The current fleet of fourteen nuclear-armed submarines could be reduced to eight. This would still allow a robust submarine-based leg of the triad but with more warheads per missile and more per submarine. The submarine leg of the triad is exceedingly survivable and as such more risk can be accepted in its size. Moreover, when existing Trident submarines and D5 missiles require replacement, the same technologies will likely be adequate, as they constitute highly survivable and reliable systems, so there should be no need for big R&D projects. Many land-based Minuteman ICBMs could be retired—at least half the current total, with more of our treaty allowance of weapons attributed to the bomber force. In fact, there is a case for eliminating all ICBMs, though I do not assume that option here.

The Department of Energy's nuclear weapons assets could be scaled back. One of the country's two main weapons laboratories, at Los Alamos or Livermore, would gradually leave the nuclear weapons business while keeping very active in other areas of modern science. No dedicated new facility to make the plutonium "pits" at the heart of most weapons would be needed, since the existing small facility at Los Alamos could be used as the arsenal continued to shrink in the years ahead. Annual savings of all the above would total about $2.5 billion.[28]

2. Reduce further spending on missile defense. Missile defense is important, and is hardly the anachronism of U.S.-

Russian nuclear competition of years gone by that critics sometimes imply. But it remains somewhat overfunded, with too many systems in various stages of development and deployment. Current programs include upgrades to the ground-based strategic systems in California and Alaska, Aegis sea-based theater defense, THAAD land-based theater defense, and two land-based short-range defense systems including the Patriot and also the MEADS program, the latter being pursued in partnership with European allies. Annual savings from canceling one of the latter two could average close to $1 billion a year over the coming decade.[29] A similar more discriminating approach to future missile defense programs thereafter could sustain such a rate of savings.

3. Apply the new concepts for global presence to the aircraft carrier fleet. As discussed above, the United States is overdue to apply new and more flexible concepts to a mission that remains very important, but can be done more efficiently. It is paramount that the Navy be able to maintain steady, continuous presence with a variety of capabilities in and about the Persian Gulf as well as the waters of the western Pacific. But this does not require a fleet of exactly the current size. A further modest reduction in the aircraft carrier fleet from eleven ships to ten, and air wings from ten to nine, would be compatible with protecting these core

interests. The resulting average annual savings would be some $2 billion. This can be done largely by further deemphasizing the need for carrier operations in the Atlantic and Mediterranean.[30] Indeed, given ship maintenance schedules, the Navy is already going to get practice in operating a fleet with only nine available carriers in the coming years, the number that would normally be ready to go with a ten-ship fleet.[31] So it will have largely adjusted to the implications of this possible permanent change.

4. Reduce surface combatants too. Rotating crews by airlift while leaving ships themselves deployed longer abroad, discussed in an earlier chapter, would also permit a slowdown in the production of large surface combatants. In this case it would be necessary to keep at least one production line warm to retain industry's skills in shipbuilding. So the savings would not be as great as otherwise hoped. But they could still average almost $1 billion a year into the future, as the average construction rate of ships currently likely to cost $1.5 billion to $2 billion each could be reduced by an average of almost one per year. Factoring in operating savings, $1 billion a year is a realistic savings target.[32]

5. Even more dramatic change is possible in a program known as the Littoral Combat Ship (LCS), designed to replace the country's frigates and some mine warfare ships. It

was supposed to be an efficient, economical vessel with innovative concepts, but has gradually evolved into something more like a traditional frigate with a half-billion-dollar price tag per vessel. Rather than build more than fifty, the Navy should adopt a new approach. One approach might be simply to cancel the LCS and buy a variant of the Coast Guard's National Security Cutter to achieve economies of scale in that program. Regardless, the Navy should consider buying just ten to twenty such vessels (either LCS or the National Security Cutter) to serve as "mother ships" for a new type of networked naval capability featuring other, cheaper vessels. Some could be low-draft high-speed ships like the Stiletto or Seahawk, which capture their own wake and thereby travel fast and efficiently along the lines of what the LCS was itself originally supposed to do. These other vessels could take advantage of new technology such as advanced mine countermeasures capabilities that can be deployed on numerous platforms besides the LCS.[33] Someday soon, more unmanned vessels could contribute to operations in shallow waters too. Resulting savings would be at least $1 billion a year in acquisition and additional amounts in reduced longer-term operating costs.

6. Reduce the purchase of the Marine Corps V-22 Osprey program. This tilt-rotor plane, which takes off and lands

like a helicopter but flies like a propeller craft, is impressive, and many of the earlier kinks have been worked out. But the added survivability it provides in battle is modest, for the simple reason that it will be exposed in the vertical parts of its flight like a helicopter. And the added cost is not worth it for routine missions, as reinforced by the fact that the Army is not buying them. Viewing the V-22 as a niche capability and instead buying existing-generation helicopters to replace aging lift capabilities would produce annual savings of nearly $1 billion for a number of years.

The list reveals the challenges—but also the feasibility—of finding big savings in acquisition accounts. Big as they are, and unpopular as they would be in some quarters, the above changes would altogether save some $15 billion each year in Pentagon spending. But $15 billion is not even quite 10 percent of the annual acquisition budget at present. Those arguing for defense cuts of 15 or 20 percent—well above what would result from even my aggressive approach to cost savings—should therefore be cautioned about the viability of the task. My list is not comprehensive, of course, and other savings could be found in the Pentagon's weapons accounts. But the above changes are aggressive and risky themselves, and push the limit of what is advisable in light of changing technologies and rising potential challengers in the international system.

CHAPTER EIGHT

Stress Testing the Force with China and Iran

Consider the following scenario that Taiwan expert Richard Bush and I discussed several years ago, and that could still easily occur. A new leader of Taiwan decides, like at least two past leaders, to pursue more autonomy. Taiwan, a high-technology land of almost 25 million, already has its own political system, economy, and military. But very few countries around the world recognize it as a nation-state out of deference to the far larger People's Republic of China. That fact tends to frustrate many of the citizens of Taiwan, and political leaders there have been known to play to this emotion. They know that simply declaring independence would be too much, angering even Washington and quite likely provoking a Chinese attack. So they try to be a bit more clever, for example making statements to the effect of "we have no need to declare independence because we already have state-to-state relations with the PRC." Many Americans sympathize with freedom-loving Taiwan and believe that the island should be able to determine its own future. The U.S. government's position is that Taiwan does not have the right simply to choose its own future unilaterally, and must work it out peacefully with China. Yet a future leader of Taiwan might get imaginative and do something that he or she thought Taiwan could get away with, in terms of pursuing moves toward independence without going so far as to provoke China into attack.

What if Beijing did not find any such action by Taiwan to be acceptable? Going beyond what happened in 1995 and 1996, when China shot missiles near the coasts of Taiwan to object to such tendencies, perhaps the next time China would do more. I do not consider a purely economic Chinese response here, which might be the more likely (and wiser) move on Beijing's part—and one that I assume should if necessary be addressed in kind by Washington, diplomatically and economically, rather than through the use of force. But in military terms, China could, for example, create a loose blockade around Taiwan until the offending president recanted the offensive action—or even stepped down from office. China might be able to pull this off with little loss of life and therefore, it might hope, little risk of direct American intervention. But what if Taipei did not back down and the crisis escalated? And what if Taiwan's economy was then slowly strangled due to Chinese actions that we interpreted as blatant aggression? Could the United States stand by while a long-standing small friend was attacked by an autocratic giant? If we did so, what message would that send to other American allies around the world, who might then doubt America's promises to help defend them if they wound up at war? Arms races and nuclear proliferation in several tense theaters could be the result.

So far my proposed force posture and weapons modernization agenda have been evaluated against ground-combat contingencies in places ranging from Korea to South Asia to the Middle East. Since ground forces like those recommended here would be similar in size and capability to those of the 1990s, when four defense secretaries and two presidents of two different parties all supported them, this proposal is forward-leaning but not radical. Moreover, since that period, one of the two most likely scenarios has gone away, in the sense that it has now already happened—the invasion and subsequent counterinsurgency and stabilization mission in Iraq. As such, a framework of "one war plus several smaller operations" to guide the sizing of the main ground combat forces of the U.S. military has reasonable historical and strategic grounding. That is as it should be, in a dangerous world.

Here, I wish to "stress test" the smaller proposed force in regard to two rising powers, China and Iran, for scenarios like the one sketched out above. In these places, no nemesis like Saddam Hussein or the Taliban regime has been swept aside. In these places, what has happened since the 1990s benchmark period has often been unfavorable to American interests.

Iran has made further progress toward possible nuclear weapons capabilities while showing its continued nefarious ways in arming Hezbollah, Hamas, and the Iraqi insurgents who killed so many Americans over the past decade. Its conventional military has atrophied in some ways due to UN sanctions, and it would probably not do well in classic large-scale military operations, either offensively or defensively. But its ability to develop special-purpose weaponry like antiship missiles and sea mines (not to mention the famous IEDs, a category of military technology in which it arguably leads the world) means that it could nonetheless prove a quite nettlesome threat in certain ways. China has roughly doubled its military spending and made huge strides in its precision-strike capabilities. In these cases, potential rivals and adversaries can be expected to watch carefully for any sign of American weakness that excessive defense cuts might portend. As such, in these places, we must be especially careful about the impact of any reductions in the military.

I do not mean to equate the nature of the Iranian and Chinese threats to American allies and interests, only to note that developments by each country raise substantial challenges for the United States. Iran is, simply put, if not an enemy then certainly at least a nemesis. Even if we have not been at war against Iran in recent years it has arguably been at war against us, sending advanced weapons like the famous "explosively formed penetrators" or EFPs, an advanced form of an improvised explosive device, into Iraq, where they killed literally hundreds of U.S. troops.

China poses a different sort of challenge altogether. Its leadership remains autocratic, but nonetheless impressive, having pulled more human beings out of poverty than any other government in the history of the planet. It is an important trade partner. It works with the United States fairly closely to address some issues of common concern such as North Korea's nuclear program, and it ultimately tends to offer real if begrudging support to the United States when dealing with other international security challenges such as Iran's nuclear weapons program. (In this latter case, the help is largely via economic sanctions applied through the

United Nations.) On balance, even as a defense analyst, I would describe China as more friend than adversary.

But if China is probably a friend, it is nonetheless a friendly rival, and an extraordinarily capable one at that whose rise to superpower status promises to shape much of twenty-first-century global politics. It is hard to believe that, despite all of its problems such as overpopulation, severe destruction of the environment, limits on fresh water availability, and ongoing major poverty, it will not become the other superpower in coming decades.[1] Its GDP is likely to reach that of the United States by mid-century or so, and its manufacturing output will soon overtake that of America with no end in sight to its emergence as the world's preeminent industrial power. Again, history teaches us that whenever such "hegemonic shifts" occur in world power distributions, the risk of war goes up as the new power jostles for position internationally with established powers. On the other side of the coin, to the extent China encounters major challenges in its development and falls short of its goals, that too may be dangerous. Out of economic desperation, or a desire to rev up nationalism to deflect its citizens' attention away from the failings of their own leaders, China may then become even more assertive in claiming disputed resources in ways that could lead to conflict with its neighbors.

This does not mean the United States should simply

China's Gross Domestic Product (Purchasing Power Parity), 1980-2010
Billions of dollars

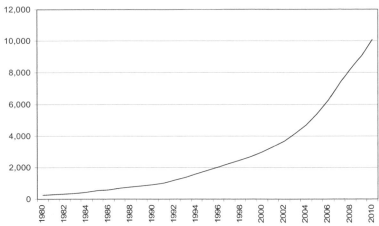

Source: The World Bank Group, World dataBank (2011), accessed at:
http://databank.worldbank.org

Purchasing Power Parity (PPP) figures are somewhat greater than GDP measured by
official nominal exchange rates. For comparison, U.S. GDP (PPP) in 2010 was 14,582 (i
billions of dollars).

**China's Gross Domestic Product (Purchasing Power Parity) as Share of World
Gross Domestic Product, 1980-2010**
Percent

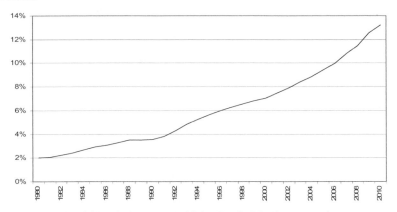

Source: The World Bank Group, World dataBank (2011), accessed at:
http://databank.worldbank.org

Purchasing Power Parity figures are somewhat greater than GDP measured by official
nominal exchange rates.

double down on its military capabilities; trying to alleviate distrust and build more cooperative patterns of interaction with China have a hugely important role too.[2] But such efforts do not always work. U.S. and allied resolve and steadiness in military capabilities are also an important element of a balanced American strategy toward China. We need to hedge against the possibility that China's rise will go badly even as we try to engage China and accord it greater status and influence in global diplomacy. That is the right prescription for minimizing the chances of war, and it is thankfully long-standing U.S. policy as well. This is not just a matter of military force planning; economic issues are central to the task as well, including limiting our dependence on key materials or products coming primarily from China (such as rare earth metals).[3] But one question is central for this book: will the new, reduced military posture of the United States be up to the associated task?

Some would counsel us to prioritize, to determine which theater is the greater priority for the United States between the Persian Gulf and western Pacific, or which challenger is the greater worry, Iran or China. But playing Russian roulette is not a sound way to do strategy unless one is forced simply to gamble. The United States has a poor track record of predicting where its next major crisis or war will result, less because of our collective lack of wisdom than because of the nature of human history. One thing that can safely be said is that, when we decide a given key region is *not* a key interest and pull back militarily or strategically, we often wind up ruing our decision—as in Europe after World War I, or Korea after World War II, or Afghanistan after the Soviets were driven out of that country. We should not go out in search of dragons to slay around the world, but neither should we close our eyes to the possibility that such dragons do exist—and that we simply cannot always know when or where they will threaten us next.

Beyond the specific cases of Iran and China, there is also a simple and compelling deterrent logic in favor of being able to respond to crisis in more than one place at once. That way, if we do wind up challenged in one location, we are less likely to be seen by other would-be adversaries as so consumed by the first problem that they can then strike elsewhere. A modified version of this logic guided my proposal for smaller ground forces—where I argued that, even if it was no longer necessary to fight two all-out ground wars at once, the United States did still need the capacity for smaller operations elsewhere as it simultaneously conducted one large combat operation. Again, this type of proper caution should not be taken to extremes. Having the capacity to respond to two major crises, not three or four, would seem adequate for the naval and air

China's Military Expenditures, 1996-2009
Billions of 2011 dollars

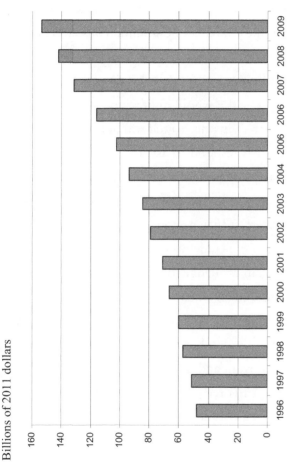

Source: U.S. Department of Defense, "Military and Security Developments Involving the People's Republic of China 2010" (Washington, August 2010), p. 42.

Estimates by the International Institute for Strategic Studies, as reported in their annual publication *The Military Balance*, are about 1/2 lower, per year, than those reported by the Department of Defense.

forces. Moreover, I do not presume that we must be able to defeat in overwhelming and rapid fashion both Chinese forces and Iranian forces at once. That would be a very demanding yardstick that we may not even be able to satisfy now. Rather, the goal must be simultaneous large-scale crisis response with the ability to win one air-naval campaign that actually does erupt into hostilities. Put differently, and looking at the whole military posture together, we need to be able to win one ground war and one maritime campaign while also responding to smaller crises on land and sea elsewhere.

The stress test applied in this chapter focuses on two specific scenarios of sufficient concern to warrant special attention. It does not include other cases that could in theory arise—a Russian challenge to a Baltic state or Georgia, China-Japan naval engagements in the East China Sea, a Venezuelan strike against Colombia, or the like. All these scenarios are credible, alas, but on balance they do not seem likely enough to warrant adding a third simultaneous operation to Navy and Air Force planning requirements. Thankfully, the United States would have some capacity to respond to any of them occurring in isolation, based on the capabilities identified here for China and Iran, but they would not be additive demands on the force.

How does one test the force against the rise of China

and the malevolence of Iran? In theory one could do detailed combat simulations for various scenarios. These have their place, and I have participated in such exercises before myself. But for current purposes, I take a simpler approach. Deterrence and U.S. warfighting ability for both these theaters today appear reasonably robust. My goal is to show that they will remain just as robust in the future. So the future proposed force posture will be measured against today's. The standards of measurement will include combat capabilities—for striking at Iran's nuclear facilities (even though I tend to think this mission would not make sense under most assumptions), keeping open the Persian Gulf to oil shipping even if Iran tries to close it, and upholding any sanctions on Iran the international community may choose to impose in the future that could require physical enforcement. For China, the main goal is to protect Taiwan, not so much against an all-out invasion threat, which I consider implausible, but against more limited uses of force such as a "leaky naval blockade" that the PRC might attempt to carry out.

At one level, a smaller and less expensive military cannot really be expected to do all the things that a larger and more robustly funded force would have done. But I have sought to propose cuts in capabilities and missions that would be less than central to the Iran and China challenges.

As such, for the most plausible and important scenarios, the alternative force posture proposed here is designed not to increase risk or reduce capability for these two important cases, and in the remaining pages I show why that should be the case.

To accomplish the missions sketched out above, the future military needs to do several things as well as today's:

• Maintain peacetime presence in the general Persian Gulf and western Pacific waters as a deterrent;

• Maintain the capacity for rapid reinforcement of normal peacetime presence in these areas as an added deterrent;

• Modernize the capabilities the United States deploys in these areas, both in peacetime and in possible crisis response operations, to counter improving Iranian and Chinese forces;

• If necessary field war-winning capabilities in one place, with enough attrition reserve to account for possible combat losses. The force packages need not necessarily be adequate to win decisively in both places at once, but they must be capable at least of pursuing one clear victory while avoiding defeat in the second place long enough to allow forces to complete the first job and then "swing" to the other theater in a worst case.

Satisfying the first requirement has already been assured by the fact that no reductions have been recommended in the base structure the United States employs in either main theater. The somewhat smaller Navy proposed above has been designed to maintain its capacities in the Persian Gulf and western Pacific as well. This is an important feature of the alternative force posture and, if adopted by American policymakers in the future, should be emphasized rhetorically a good deal—both to remind potential adversaries and to reassure allies. Forward presence in and near key waters will not decline.

It is true that the drawdown from Iraq has greatly reduced the numbers of American forces in the Persian Gulf. But those forces were never there for regional power projection. On balance, they were more of a drag on America's strategic position than an advantage (though they were necessary for stabilizing Iraq for a time, to be sure). Yes, some intelligence capabilities may have been embedded within the American forces, and those may have to be replaced in some way with the modest addition of capabilities along certain other parts of the Gulf. But the changes in main combat forces should be fine—as long as robust Navy capabilities remain as before in the Gulf and as long as the capacity to deploy tactical combat aircraft quickly in countries like Kuwait, Qatar, the UAE, and Saudi Arabia remains.

Similarly, the possible relocation of about half of American Marine forces presently on Okinawa to Guam might cause some concern. But Guam remains close to the theater in question, and those Marines always had limited capacity for crisis response in the region in any event given their lack of lift assets nearby. So the Guam change, if it happens, will not affect the big picture. It is important that Tokyo and Washington avoid a row over the Okinawa issue, and it would be preferable that the allies stop consuming so much of the oxygen in their relationship on this tired issue and find a mutually acceptable solution. But none of the plans in consideration would weaken American presence in the Pacific, so in broader terms all of them (as well as the status quo) are in fact acceptable. If the Guam Marine Corps relocation plan is canceled as I recommend, U.S. response capabilities would actually improve with the addition of prepositioned equipment aboard ships ready to move out quickly from Japanese ports.

Regardless, homeporting an aircraft carrier battle group in Japan and basing two wings of fighter aircraft there and a similar number in Korea will continue. Ideally, capabilities on Guam for attack submarines and aircraft will expand as I have recommended here, and be protected by increased hardening of facilities against attack. Recent purchases of aircraft such as the F-18E/F Super Hornet (for aircraft carriers) as well as the F-22 and, soon, the F-35 will ensure that increasingly top-rate combat forces can be deployed in these zones.

Satisfying the second requirement above is largely a matter of having adequate mobility, plus local base capacity in the Persian Gulf and western Pacific that can receive and support reinforcements. Regarding the mobility, America's strategic lift including ships and airplanes is currently strong and should remain that way. Since early in the Cold War, and particularly since the Soviet invasion of Afghanistan, the United States has placed a high premium on such mobility. Indeed, lift has improved since the end of the Cold War, a signature accomplishment of the Clinton administration that built on work of previous governments and was sustained thereafter by George W. Bush.

Among its other capabilities, the United States has about three dozen amphibious ships capable of carrying more than two brigades of Marines and their equipment. It has roughly 360 large airplanes for carrying troops and equipment, as well as another 200 quickly available via the civil reserve air fleet program. Each is typically able to carry around 50 tons of cargo per flight.[4] This number of planes may in fact be slightly in excess of needs, as the C-17 aircraft production line has been kept open by Congress somewhat longer than required. Finally, the United States now possesses about 20 large "roll-on roll-off" ships, each capable of carrying 15,000 to 20,000 tons of equipment (equipment and initial supplies for a heavy division weigh about 100,000 tons). Altogether, these assets create a theoretical capacity for a sustained average movement of about 30,000 tons of military equipment a day.[5]

Despite the possibility for some efficiencies, it is important to retain most of these capacities. They are important for ground force scenarios like those discussed in chapter 5, and for Pacific or Persian Gulf maritime crises being considered here. A smaller force must remain an agile, mobile, rapidly deployable military.

Regarding the third goal, adequate modernization, how does the smaller and leaner military proposal stack up? The key here is to note that what matters less than total capabilities based back in the United States is those capabilities that can be deployed to the Pacific and Persian Gulf theaters and operated there. Land bases in these two areas accessible to the United States might hold 300 to 500 tactical aircraft. Normally, two carriers are deployed in these two areas as well, with another 150 planes or so. Two large-deck amphibious ships have capacity for up to another 50, if suitably configured, for a total of 500 planes at sea. Surge forces for the two theaters should include several hundred more planes, presuming for example a doubling of the carrier presence in both places and related steps with land bases. So the United States needs some 1,000 tactical aircraft for this purpose. The 189 F-22 planes already bought and 1,250 F-35 that would be bought under my proposal would suffice, not even including the increased new role of drones and the evolving role of bombers carrying precision-strike munitions. They could not only maintain air superiority over open waters and around Taiwan, but provide the potential to strike at Chinese air bases and ports as well. Additional capabilities could be provided by existing aircraft like F-15s and F-16s, though in regard to China in particular it would be preferable to use stealthy aircraft to the maximum extent feasible. Modernization of munitions and reconnaissance platforms is also important and should be sustained. It is often such lower-profile and less costly capabilities that provide the United States its most potent fighting capabilities.

Beyond these offensive weapons, more defensive capabilities are surely needed. We are in an era of growing threat to large and fixed or relatively slow-moving, military assets like airfields and aircraft carriers that the United States has relied upon to maintain its leverage in overseas theaters for decades. It is too soon to know if such assets will become simply indefensible, but the trends are certainly working against them now. Specific Chinese modernizations like the

DF-21 ballistic missile and DH-10 land attack cruise missile and Russian-built SS-N-27B antiship cruise missile are particularly significant.[6] China is also making progress underwater with submarine technologies, providing more ambush and surprise-attack capabilities that will be difficult to counter.[7] In a sense, that is a return to what has been historically normal; the United States has grown accustomed to operating its major naval and air capabilities largely with impunity, and that set of circumstances will not last.

A host of responses are needed. As noted, we need aircraft that can use smaller airfields, partially damaged airfields, and even roads or fields as alternatives to long runways. We need more runway repair equipment, hardened aircraft shelters, underground fuel and ordnance storage systems, and the like. Missile defenses have a role too, even if they will have a hard time stopping more than a certain percentage of incoming threats given the laws of statistics. As part of any decision to downsize its military, the United States and regional allies must continue to upgrade these kinds of capabilities to reinforce their resoluteness and signal their seriousness about prevailing in future conflicts. The effort should focus not only on major American military installations in Asia and the Persian Gulf, but other facilities too—Japanese commercial airfields, perhaps Filipino airfields, and possibly other places as well.

Finally, what about actual warfighting? Of course this issue depends acutely on the scenario in question. But a relatively stressing case would be a protracted Chinese effort to prevent seaborne commerce in and out of Taiwan. Beijing's idea might be to use a combination of missile strikes against ports, cyberattacks, and ultimately submarines shooting torpedoes or antiship missiles at cargo ships to complicate the ability of any company or foreign entity to trade with Taiwan. By sinking just a few ships and introducing major danger into the voyages of others, China might effectively sink the Taiwanese economy at relatively low risk to itself and at relatively low cost in lives. Indeed, China could even try to rescue seamen from the ships it attacked to prove its "humane" ways and thereby limit the risk of international retribution. Such a scenario would be far more promising for Beijing than an all-out attack and yet potentially almost as effective in cowing Taipei. China might further hope that its antiship capabilities would deter American involvement.

In previous work, I have estimated what the United States might need to do in response, working with Taiwan's military to protect sea and air lanes into and out of Taiwan so that normal commerce could resume. I calculated that we would need a force of up to four aircraft carrier battle groups, reinforced tactical combat airpower on Okinawa and perhaps also the Philippines, and a range of other assets including attack submarines and maritime patrol aircraft—the latter especially important since China might start shooting down American satellites in low-Earth orbit in this kind of engagement. Moreover, I estimated that perhaps 10 to 25 percent of deployed American assets could be lost in such a campaign. In addition, the scenario could last long enough that a "rotation base" would be needed to allow forces to go home periodically for a rest and for equipment maintenance, being replaced by fresh units as required.

All told, in a worst case, this scenario could require the entire recommended fleet of ten aircraft carriers if it lasted long enough and led to damage or attrition of one or two of them. In other words, eight carriers to sustain the four-carrier presence indefinitely, plus one or two more in case anything was lost or damaged. That is a worst-case assessment, and if it happened, we could probably find ways to get by without carriers in the Persian Gulf through the temporary use of more land-based airpower. But it is the kind of assessment that underscores the importance of not cutting existing capabilities too deeply.

Another plausible scenario would be extended operations to enforce sanctions, perhaps against Iran.[8] Or perhaps a demining operation might be needed in the Gulf after Iran laid sea mines to prevent other countries from using the waters, and threatened missile strikes against any transiting vessels as well. For the latter scenario, one analyst estimates that in addition to mine countermeasures ships, the United States would need multiple Aegis-class surface combatants, at least one carrier battle group, and two to three fighter squadrons.[9]

In fact, with an acute risk of hostilities, the United States would in my judgment want at least two carrier battle groups to allow each ship some downtime (avoiding the need for indefinite, twenty-four-hour-a-day operations) and also provide some capacity for reinforcement. Carrying out that Persian Gulf mission while simultaneously maintaining routine presence in the Pacific would require three carriers on station indefinitely. That could be handled for a period, but would be at the outer bounds of what a ten-carrier fleet could sustain for one to more years. Such a scenario argues against deeper cuts in the carrier force and other Navy assets, since ships provide greater flexibility and additional coverage that land-based assets cannot always provide. That is especially true now, as the overthrow of Saddam's regime in Iraq has led to a major drawdown in those tactical combat aircraft once based in places such as Saudi Arabia and Kuwait.

Scenario analysis is of course always dependent on the specific conditions assumed. But a stress test of the somewhat smaller force shows that it can indeed handle most plausible peacetime, crisis, and combat demands that would be placed upon it in the western Pacific and Persian Gulf. We can find clever ways to sustain our capabilities in these two crucial and turbulent theaters even with a smaller military if we make our cuts carefully. This will not be a permanent solution to the challenges posed by China. Some worry that in a decade or so military trends could turn further against America's ability to help protect Taiwan, another reminder of the importance of not making cutbacks too precipitously at this important moment in world history.[10] But then again, the United States continues to outinvest China substantially in overall military technology and could continue to do so even at the lower budget levels discussed here, as long as cutbacks allow for continued innovation in cutting-edge technologies, such as unmanned aerial vehicles and precision strike capabilities.

On balance, Pentagon budget reductions of some 8 to 10 percent may be viable. But deeper cuts in American military spending and American combat forces would introduce risks that seem excessive in light of the plausible threats and challenges to U.S. global interests in the years ahead.

CHAPTER NINE

Intelligence, Homeland Security, Diplomacy, Democracy, and Development

T his book is mostly about U.S. defense spending. It is one of four giants in the federal budget, along with Medicare, Medicaid, and Social Security. All other domestic programs combined, things like science research, infrastructure construction, and federal support for education that are found within the so-called domestic discretionary account, could be called a fifth giant—but only if they are so lumped together. And defense constitutes the predominant expense in American foreign and national security policy. But there are other elements to those broader policies that deserve some consideration here—mostly because they are not funded as well as defense, and as such are in need of greater relative protection in the budget process. They have also been lumped together with military spending by the August 2011 debt deal. With the exception perhaps of the intelligence, and to a lesser extent the homeland security budgets, they also tend not to have the political champions that the armed forces enjoy. That is one more reason they need to be discussed.

The budgets of these other elements of American power total about $75 billion for intelligence, some $45 billion for homeland security, and another $60 billion for the combined activities of diplomacy, democracy promotion, and development.

Actually, most of the intelligence budget is found within the U.S. military budget. There is no getting around the fact that it is quite large—bigger in fact than any other country's entire military budget with the possible exception of China's. It has also more than doubled over the last dozen years or so, to the extent that occasional public disclosures of its aggregate size allow such comparisons to be made. The CIA added 50 percent more operations officers and analysts after 9/11.[1] Related efforts like the FBI's have grown too, driven by a 100 percent increase in national security–oriented agents.[2] Unfortunately, in the interest of secrecy, little additional information is commonly provided to understand how the budget breaks down among the intelligence community's seventeen organizations—from the CIA to the National Security Agency to the National Geospatial-Intelligence Agency to the Defense Intelligence Agency, as well as the intelligence units of each military service and each unified geographic command.[3]

The intelligence world has come under criticism in recent years, some of it deserved, for a number of failings. It did not synthesize and understand the various warnings that a major attack was in the making prior to 9/11 in a way that allowed it to "connect the dots" and perhaps help prevent the attack. Its incorrect view that Saddam had weapons of mass destruction, and its on-again/off-again warnings about Iran's progress toward a possible nuclear weapons capability, have complicated American foreign policy and caused major fallout. But it is also important to recall that intelligence is an inherently difficult and uncertain business, as much of it concerns trying to read other people's minds and to predict the future. As Columbia University professor Richard Betts has persuasively argued, without trying to whitewash the record of the American intelligence community, critics of intelligence often forget this important point and impose unrealistic expectations on a business that cannot be expected to have a perfect track record.[4]

To put the situation in perspective, it is worth quoting from General David Petraeus's June 2011 testimony before the Senate when seeking confirmation to become the CIA's next director. Petraeus said the following: "The professionals of the Agency are our country's best and brightest, men and women who voluntarily undertake some of the most difficult tasks for our Nation, men and women for whom integrity in analysis is the watchword. I have served closely with many of them since 9/11, and I cannot say enough about them and the sacrifices they and their families make for our country."[5] These words of high praise from one of our nation's greatest generals ring sincere, and remind us of the need not to throw the baby out with the bathwater when trying to repair or reform intelligence.

In addition to its challenges in regard to terrorism, the intelligence community also has taken on new tasks in recent years such as addressing the huge growth in cybersecurity concerns; it also has to contend with the growing vulnerability of its space assets owing to trends in technology.[6] And at a time of uncertainty in the international environment due to the rise of many new powers, its overall activities remain at least as important as ever.

Yet some of the expansion of intelligence capabilities may have gone too far. The Defense Intelligence Agency more than doubled in size over the last decade. A multitude of new organizations was created. And far more contractors were hired to support these efforts. Various officials and former officials from the intelligence world consider much of the growth since 9/11 to have been justifiable but some to have been excessive. So significant belt tightening is indeed appropriate in the intelligence world.[7]

One thing that would *not* be wise would be to conduct yet another reorganization effort, following the recent one of 2004. These reorganizations are symbolically appealing ways to "do something" after failures, but they tend to disrupt activities and distract from the hard work of identifying and tracking threats more than they help. Specifically, the 2004 effort probably did at least as much harm as good. It created a new director of intelligence who, because he no longer ran the CIA, lacked a strong institutional base and may have thereby actually lost rather than gained clout, even as one more layer was added to the intelligence bureaucracy.[8]

Before leaving office, and before the intensity of deficit reduction efforts so dramatically picked up, Secretary of Defense Gates had already set a goal to reduce the contractor workforce by a total of 30 percent over three years—largely a product of its growth in intelligence-related fields. That goal, already factored into previous defense budget reduction efforts, makes sense—and may be ambitious enough a savings target for now. It is possible that the intelligence community is pursuing too many big-ticket items like expensive satellites but it is difficult to know that from the public record.

As General Petraeus again put it, to me personally this time, after being briefed on the CIA's budget he was struck by how relatively modest it was in size. He further commented that it must be one of the best bargains the country is getting from its government. He may have an interest in arguing that, to be sure, but he is a notoriously direct person, and the comments were clearly sincere. Nor is General Petraeus the first to feel that way. On balance, carrying out the Gates reforms while saving at most a couple billion dollars more in annual satellite-related expenses from the broader intelligence community would seem an ambitious goal that we will do well to achieve. Intelligence probably should not be cut by quite as great a proportion as other elements of national security spending. Perhaps the resulting yearly budget can be reduced to $70 billion from its current level of around $75 billion.

The nation's homeland security efforts represent a reorganization and expansion of many activities that used to occur under other agencies before 9/11. The Department of

State-Foreign Operations Appropriations
Billions of constant 2011 dollars

Year	2002	2003	2004	2005	2006	2007	2008	2009	2010	2011	2012
2011 $	30.8	39.3	58.2	39.8	38.4	40.7	42.6	52.9	56.8	49.8	59.7

Source: Susan B. Epstein, "State, Foreign Operations, and Related Programs: FY2012 Budget and Appropriations" (Washington: Congressional Research Service, August 2011), p. 12

Figures include all previously enacted appropriations.

Composition of the State-Foreign Operations Budget Request, FY2012

Bilateral Economic Aid	39%
State Administrative Costs	25%
Security Aid	19%
International Organizations	6%
Multilateral Aid	6%
USAID Administrative Costs	3%
International Broadcasting	1%
Millenium Challenge Corporation	1%

Source: Susan B. Epstein, "State, Foreign Operations, and Related Programs: FY2012 Budget and Appropriations" (Washington: Congressional Research Service, August 2011), p. 3

Homeland Security now includes the Federal Emergency Management Agency, the Coast Guard, the Transportation Security Administration, and many others. Today, the Department of Homeland Security spends about three times what the various component agencies now making it up used to spend each year, before 9/11.

Interestingly, this spending figure of about $45 billion a year has plateaued for about half a decade. After a major increase in the years right after the September 11, 2001, attacks, things slowed down as a rough form of consensus appeared to develop across the political spectrum. Indeed, the Obama administration has not radically changed the budget levels or overall programmatic emphasis of DHS since taking over in 2009.

To the extent one can explain the consensus, it appears to reflect a general agreement that we must do more than before to protect ourselves against the most likely threats, especially in areas like aviation where al-Qaeda has attacked in the past. But at the same time, we should not threaten our collective way of life or turn the nation into a virtual fortress by defending ourselves robustly against hypothetical attacks of many different types. For example, outside of New York most cities have done relatively little to develop organic counterterrorism units, trains and subways remain fairly lightly guarded, major buildings apart from iconic symbols like the Empire State Building have not for the most part greatly improved their resilience to attack, and the nation's overall approach to preparing to address chemical or biological attack has been targeted rather than sweeping. Books like *America the Vulnerable* and *Open Target* that continued to sound the clarion call of national vulnerability a few years ago generally have not produced a new wave of big programs or spending initiatives.[9]

For the most part, this is to the good. Rolling up terrorists abroad and making it harder for them to enter the United States—preventive efforts—generally make more sense than battening down the hatches throughout the country. And we have made enough inroads with offensive operations abroad, as well as better integration of terrorist watch lists and closer vigilance regarding people entering the United States, that hardening the country comprehensively is not necessary or desirable.

That said, there are areas where we probably still do not do enough. Since 9/11, the Coast Guard has devoted at least 25 percent of its mission hours to counterterrorism but grown in size only 15 percent; this mismatch should probably be rectified with a larger fleet. New York's efforts to build dedicated counterterrorism capabilities, as well as better monitoring of its subway system, should be emulated by other big cities at proportionate scales. Given the dangers inherent in attack by biological pathogens, which will only become more dangerous in the decades ahead, we need better detectors as well as the capacity to make antidote and treat victims quickly and on a large scale. Even if 100 percent physical screening is unnecessary, a higher percentage of cargo traffic entering the United States (and leaving, especially to Mexico) should be checked for contraband, small arms, and weapons of mass destruction. Better monitoring of trucks carrying hazardous materials within the United States makes sense too, to include safer places for such trucks to park and spend the night, automatic tracking devices in case the trucks are stolen, and related technologies. Major progress could be made on the above set of initiatives for a reasonably modest cost of perhaps $2 billion to $3 billion a year.[10]

Finding these additional dollars will be difficult in an age of austerity. Some efficiencies can surely be wrung out of the homeland security arena, given how fast growth has occurred in recent years. However, we should avoid cutting back these accounts excessively and disproportionately in the years ahead. My point is less to argue for budgetary increases than to warn against big cutbacks as part of an unbalanced effort at national deficit reduction that could occur, for example, in the event of sequestration.

The diplomacy, democracy, and aid accounts represent

yet another element of national power. Historically, they have been underfunded—so much so that former secretary of defense Gates used to go about lobbying that they should be increased even if his own department's budget was asked to foot part of the bill. And indeed, after years of effort that began under President Clinton and accelerated under President Bush and President Obama, bipartisan efforts finally began to repair the shortfalls in these areas. More foreign service officers with key language skills and other types of expertise were hired, well-performing developing countries able to make good use of development funds were given more assistance or at least helped with their preexisting debt burdens, global health programs were beefed up to deal more effectively with the scourges of AIDS, malaria, and routine malnutrition. As such, we should bear Gates's admonition in mind in the future. We should not wantonly undo what we have waited so long finally to carry out in these important areas of the nation's foreign and national security policies.

Some reductions and some reprogramming of existing funds may be acceptable. A certain amount of foreign aid is still wasted on countries that make poor use of it. Indeed, statistical analyses by analysts at the World Bank and elsewhere showed that, into the 1990s at least, on balance aid's effects were good for extending human life expectancies but insignificant for fostering global economic growth. For every star performer like South Korea that made great use of assistance, there were others that used aid to put off reforms and actually made less progress with foreign aid than they might have made without it!

However, this situation has begun to change. For example, the Bush administration created an entity called the Millennium Challenge Corporation designed to target more American aid resources to countries with good enough economic policy frameworks to make profitable use of them. Private investment flows are reinforcing these improvements in aid in many places, and the results are coming in.[11] On balance, there are many more good performers these days in the developing world, and hundreds of millions of people are being lifted out of poverty and despair as a result. And Bush, like Clinton before him and Obama after, realized the challenge posed by global health threats like HIV/AIDS, leading to bipartisan accord to increase resources for activities designed to address them. There are security benefits to such improvements too, as terrorists often benefit from sanctuaries located in weak or failed states, and as outside powers often have to respond with expensive and protracted operations. An ounce of prevention in these areas is truly worth a pound of cure.

There has been progress with the State Department

and related agencies too. In much of the 1990s budgets went down, even as the number of countries in the world requiring diplomatic attention went up. But that has changed. Recommendations by distinguished task forces to increase the number of State Department foreign service officers, as well as AID foreign service officers, by one thousand each are on the road to fruition.[12] These initiatives would take their combined strength from eight thousand to ten thousand, still only about half the size of a single Army infantry division.

Cutting back on budgets now would threaten these goals. It would also jeopardize President Obama's provisional success in increasing funds for global nuclear safety and nonproliferation efforts. It would also impede consideration of good ideas like that of scholar Kristin Lord to increase dramatically foreign scholarship and exchange programs and establish more American centers abroad, in an effort to improve America's image and standing throughout much of the world. Finally, it could compromise our efforts to reach out to reformers in places like Egypt who are trying to promote democracy in their own countries. With the right resources at the right time, usually in modest amounts, America can help them at a crucial moment and increase the odds of forming strong partnerships with them in the future.

Aid and diplomacy resources may not need to go up further, but it would be counterproductive to cut them very much as part of deficit reduction efforts. Since the fiscal framework of the 2011 debt deal lumps aid and diplomacy together with homeland security and defense, this risk of reductions is real. Defense spending can be cut up to 10 percent, but other elements of national power and foreign policy should be cut less if at all.

CHAPTER TEN

Conclusion

merica today is a wounded giant. But she is also a giant that the international system needs. And she can be healed.

Some scholars argue that the United States is in decline. That is correct in some specific ways; as a percentage of global economic output, American GDP is less than before and will remain that way. However, this is a narrow and ultimately incorrect way to assess the country's overall international position. On balance, declinists are more wrong than right. Or perhaps the better way to look at it is that they can still be proven wrong, if as in the past Americans respond to the crises and challenges of the day with appropriate action. Defense spending reductions as part of comprehensive deficit reduction can be an important element of such action, helping restore the nation's economic fundamentals to support a robust foreign and national security policy in the decades to come.

The United States has achieved many if not most of its post–World War II aims. The world we see today is a reflection of its foreign policy successes, not its failures. Most of the world's wealth and strength is found among its allies or friendly neutrals. The international system works well for most major countries, and even would-be challengers like China or Russia are unlikely to see much benefit in challenging it fundamentally. By embracing its successes—and the diffusion of global power that they have helped produce—the United States can probably do what no global superpower has ever done before and remain as strong as ever even as power disperses somewhat. That said, it can do so if its responses are proportionate to the challenges ahead.

The risks of doing this wrong are significant enough that I do not favor military cuts for their own sake. In fact they are difficult, and risky. They make sense only as part of a broader national effort of deficit reduction and economic renewal. My premise is that we are now perhaps taking larger security risks with our fiscal policies than with our military policies. As such, the suggestions here are motivated not by any antidefense agenda but rather by the goal of minimizing aggregate national security risk. There is no logic to enacting defense cuts if entitlement policy, tax policy, and other federal programs remain unchecked while the Pentagon is offered up as a sacrificial lamb in an unbalanced deficit reduction effort. However, done as part of a general national agenda of shared sacrifice, cuts of the requisite magnitude in defense may be feasible without requiring strategic retrenchment.

Saving 8 to 10 percent in the annual "peacetime" defense budget of the United States—arguably the Pentagon's fair share of a serious deficit reduction effort—would be hard but not impossible within such a philosophy. That would translate into $350 billion to $500 billion in aggregate ten-year cuts, to use the accounting framework that has become popular as part of the August 2011 debt deal between President Obama and the Congress. These cuts go beyond those already expected as part of a gradual reduction in the nation's costs for waging war abroad.

It would be a mistake to place the full burden of finding around $50 billion in additional annual savings, beyond those already identified in recent times by Secretary Gates, within any one functional area of the defense establishment. The future risks facing the United States, and thus the future missions facing the American military, are too disparate and too hard to predict. Management reforms, force structure cuts, and weapons modernization reductions would all have to contribute.

Larger defense cuts that could approach $1 trillion over ten years would be unwise. The smaller ones discussed in this book, and already largely mandated by the first effects of the August 2011 deficit reduction law, will be hard enough and risky enough. Yes, America's armed forces today are expensive, but that is for a good reason—they are a stabilizing element in the current global environment. Most other countries welcome American military power, and choose to ally with it formally or informally, even as they sometimes complain about U.S. foreign policy. And if the military is expensive, that is also because you get what you pay for. While America's armed forces are costly on a per-person basis—which is the right policy, since a democracy with an all-volunteer force owes it to men and women in uniform to take good care of them—they are not particularly large in size.

With reductions of up to 10 percent in U.S. defense spending, we can avoid salary cuts for our troops and any display of weakening resolve toward East Asia or the Persian Gulf. We can modernize forces enough that our most promising new technologies can be pursued in numbers adequate to equip the forces most likely to fight in those key regions. We can retain ground forces large enough, even after the Afghanistan campaign winds down, to carry out another war if necessary (heaven forbid) without having to let down our guard simultaneously in every other part of the world, stealing forces from all other theaters to conduct the combat operation.

It is important to remember that cutting the defense budget 8 to 10 percent in real terms implies the need for slightly greater reductions in combat forces. That is because certain economies of scale are weakened with a smaller military. It is also because some capabilities, such as strategic lift, should not be proportionately cut in any drawdown plan given their relative importance. Such lift has never been oversized in American military history and has rarely been fully capable of deploying a full contingent of combat forces even to a single war within desired time frames.

If instead we pursued defense budget cuts of 15 to 20 percent, as implied by ten-year defense savings plans that approached $1 trillion in cumulative magnitude, these would require us not just to reform military health care and retirement but to cut pay, according to my best estimates. They would force us to choose between stabilizing the Persian Gulf and stabilizing the western Pacific/East Asia region as our primary effort. They would probably require outright cancellation of some weapons programs that, while expensive, do buy us important capabilities in areas such as precision strike and stealth—needed not just to improve the military, but to sustain our current advantages over would-be rivals and redress our existing Achilles' heels. And that American military advantage over others is, despite all our foibles and failings, an unambiguously desirable feature of the current global power balance—not only for our own interests but for the overwhelming majority of other countries, who continue to enjoy an international system that is mostly free of interstate war despite its many other challenges.

Budget cuts of 15 to 20 percent would require us to cut back ground force levels below where they were in the 1990s—a capability that was itself later proven inadequate for the challenges of the following decade. They would leave the Navy too small to respond to what could be protracted crises in both the western Pacific and the Persian Gulf, even if more innovative methods of ship deployments were employed. They could lead to a situation in which American defense industry no longer could provide competition for contracts in key areas like shipbuilding and even aircraft manufacturing, as key companies would go under at a time when we are often down to just two or three firms capable of building a given product as things stand. They would so squeeze budgets that, if new needs emerged or vulnerabilities in America's military became apparent, we might be unable to develop new programs to respond.

If we got lucky internationally, and the world stayed fairly peaceful, the sky might not fall even after such reductions in American military strength. But if dark clouds loomed abroad, we would have to hope that we never faced more than one challenge at a time, and that we could address it and eliminate its cause fairly quickly. Alas, hoping for such a world is highly optimistic, and not within our power to ensure.

In the end, the United States can and should consider up to a 10 percent reduction in the expected annual cost of the nation's armed forces—with associated ten-year savings of $350 billion to $500 billion relative to earlier expectations. It should do so, however, only in the context of reestablishing national sacrifice and fiscal discipline across the government. The national security risks associated with the proposed cuts would otherwise be too great. This is a crucial guidepost for the work of the congressional supercommittee charged with the task of finding a comprehensive deficit reduction plan in 2011, the Congress as it evaluates that supercommittee's work, the presidential candidates for 2012, and the American people as we collectively evaluate the candidates' plans. One final watchword in these efforts for all of us may be that, while we rightly hold candidates and the Congress accountable for our decisions, we also hold ourselves to the basic standard that it is not right to expect government services without paying for them and not right to leave huge fiscal and economic woes to our children and grandchildren. But nor is it wise to squander the international peace and stability paid for in so many dollars and so much blood by this and previous generations.

ACKNOWLEDGMENTS

I would like to begin by thanking Brookings colleagues—Ian Livingston for research assistance and help with graphical materials, Ted Piccone for guiding the review process, Steve Pifer and Bruce Riedel and Peter Singer and Richard Bush as well as Jonathan Pollack and Clara O'Donnell for reading part or all of the draft, as well as additional inspiration and guidance from Martin Indyk, Ken Lieberthal, Ken Pollack, and Robert Kagan. Colleagues in other parts of Brookings have been hugely helpful too, starting with Alice Rivlin and Ron Haskins, and including also Bruce Katz, Amy Liu, Barry Bosworth, Bill Gale, Belle Sawhill, Gary Burtless, Henry Aaron, William Galston, Rebecca Winthrop, and Carol Graham. Outside of Brookings, Maya MacGuineas and Bob Reischauer have as always taught me a great deal about the budget, as have Stephen Biddle, Michael Berger, Wayne Glass, Lane Pierrot, Fran Lussier, David Mosher, Rachel Schmidt, Ellen Breslin-Davidson, Jack Mayer, Bob Hale, as well as Scott Moyers, my editor at The Penguin Press, and his assistant, Emily Graff. I would like to thank the Sasakawa Peace Foundation as well as Herb Allen, Marshall Rose, Casey Wasserman, Mala Gaonkar, and several anonymous donors for important support. Ari Roth and many of my students at Johns Hopkins University have helped enormously at an intellectual level as well. And I'd like to dedicate this e-book to two members of the e-generation, my great daughters Lily and Grace, as well as their awesome mother Cathy.

Notes

Preface

1. See for example, Amy Belasco, *Paying for Military Readiness and Upkeep: Trends in Operation and Maintenance Spending* (Washington, D.C.: Congressional Budget Office, 1997).
2. See Kathy Roth-Douquet and Frank Schaeffer, *AWOL: The Unexcused Absence of America's Upper Classes from Military Service—and How It Hurts Our Country* (New York: Collins, 2006).
3. For a good discussion of democratic peace theory, see John M. Owen, *Liberal Peace, Liberal War* (Ithaca, N.Y.: Cornell University Press, 1997).
4. See for example, "French Embrace of NATO's Power Is Huge Step for World," Bloomberg View, August 30, 2011, available at http://www.businessweek.com/news/2011-08-30/french-embrace-of-nato-s-power-is-huge-step-for-world-view.html [accessed September 22, 2011].
5. Mark Fitzpatrick, ed., *North Korean Security Challenges: A Net Assessment* (London: International Institute for Strategic Studies, 2011), pp. 47–64.

Chapter One: Introduction

1. See also Michael Mandelbaum, *The Frugal Superpower: America's Global Leadership in a Cash-Strapped Era* (New York: Public Affairs, 2010).
2. On China's rise, and how the United States should respond, see for example Ashton B. Carter and William J. Perry, *Preventive Defense: A New Security Strategy for America* (Washington, D.C.: Brookings, 1999), pp. 92–122; and C. Fred Bergsten, Charles Freeman, Nicholas

R. Lardy, and Derek J. Mitchell, *China's Rise: Challenges and Opportunities* (Washington, D.C.: Peterson Institute for International Economics and CSIS, 2008), pp. 226–29.

3. John D. Steinbruner, *Principles of Global Security* (Washington, D.C.: Brookings, 2000).

4. See for example Stephen Biddle, *Military Power: Explaining Victory and Defeat in Modern Battle* (Princeton, N.J.: Princeton University Press, 2004), pp. 1–77. Biddle's theory applies most directly to militaries of disparate technological sophistication, but Taiwan is capable of making enough mistakes in its military preparations that it could prove vulnerable itself, as discussed further below.

5. See, for example, Jan van Tol, *AirSea Battle: A Point-of-Departure Operational Concept* (Washington, D.C.: Center for Strategic and Budgetary Assessments, 2010); Andrew F. Krepinevich, *7 Deadly Scenarios* (New York: Bantam Books, 2009), pp. 169–209; Roger Cliff, Mark Burles, Michael S. Chase, Derek Eaton, and Kevin L. Pollpeter, *Entering the Dragon's Lair* (Santa Monica, Calif.: RAND, 2007); and Stuart E. Johnson and Duncan Long, eds., *Coping with the Dragon* (Washington, D.C.: National Defense University, 2007).

6. See, for example, John Keegan, *The First World War* (New York: Alfred A. Knopf, 1999), pp. 10–18.

7. On climate change, for example, see Dr. Kurt M. Campbell et al., *The Age of Consequences: The Foreign Policy and National Security Implications of Global Climate Change* (Washington, D.C.: Center for a New American Security, November 1, 2007), available at http://www.cnas.org/files/documents/publications/CSIS-CNAS_AgeofConsequences_November07.pdf [accessed August 8, 2011]; for a very good short book on the biological weapons risk, see Richard Danzig, *Preparing for Catastrophic Bioterrorism: Toward a Long-Term Strategy for Limiting the Risk* (Washington, D.C.: Center for Technology and National Security Policy, 2008).

8. See, for example, Secretary of State Hillary Rodham Clinton, "Remarks on United States Foreign Policy," Council on Foreign Relations, Washington, D.C., September 8, 2010, available at www.state.gov/secretary/rm/2010/09/146917.htm [accessed September 10,

2010]; Speech by Secretary of Defense Robert Gates at the Eisenhower Library, Abilene, Kansas, May 8, 2010, available at www.defense.gov/speeches/speech.aspx?speechid=1467 [accessed September 10, 2010]; and Remarks by Admiral Mike Mullen at the Detroit Economic Club Luncheon, August 26, 2010, available at www.jcs.mil/speech.aspx?ID=1445 [accessed September 10, 2010].

9. "Admiral Mike Mullen: 'National Debt Is Our Biggest Security Threat," *Huffington Post*, June 24, 2010, available at http://www .huffingtonpost.com/2010/06/24/adm-mike-mullen-national_n_624096 .html [accessed November 8, 2010].

10. Richard Haass of the Council on Foreign Relations coined this phrase; see for example Richard N. Haass, *War of Necessity, War of Choice* (New York: Simon and Schuster, 2009).

11. Office of Management and Budget, *Historical Tables: Budget of the U.S. Government, Fiscal Year 2011* (Washington, D.C.: Government Printing Office, 2010), p. 146.

12. International Institute for Strategic Studies, *The Military Balance 2010* (Oxfordshire, UK: Routledge, 2010), p. 468.

13. Office of Management and Budget, *Historical Tables*, pp. 62, 83.

14. Joshua M. Epstein, "Dynamic Analysis and the Conventional Balance in Europe," *International Security*, vol. 12, no. 4 (Spring 1988), p. 156; T. N. Dupuy, *Understanding War: History and Theory of Combat* (New York: Paragon, 1987), pp. 174–80.

15. Geoffrey Blainey, *The Causes of War* (New York: Free Press, 1973), pp. 248–49.

Chapter Two: Deficits, Debt, and the Decline of Great Powers

1. Thucydides, *History of the Peloponnesian War* (New York: Penguin Books, 1986); Sun Tzu, *The Art of War* (London: Oxford University Press, 1963); Andrew F. Krepinevich, "From Cavalry to Computer: The Pattern of Military Revolutions," *The National Interest* (Fall 1994); Stephen Biddle, *Military Power* (Princeton, N.J.: Princeton University Press, 2004); Martin van Creveld, *Technology and War*

(New York: Free Press, 1991); and Max Boot, *War Made New: Technology, Warfare, and the Course of History, 1500 to Today* (New York: Gotham Books, 2006).

2. Paul Kennedy, *The Rise and Fall of the Great Powers* (New York: Random House, 1987), pp. xvii–xviii, 99.

3. Ibid., p. 199.

4. Aaron L. Friedberg, *The Weary Titan: Britain and the Experience of Relative Decline, 1895–1905* (Princeton, N.J.: Princeton University Press, 1988), pp. 26, 303.

5. See Clifford G. Gaddy, *The Price of the Past: Russia's Struggle with the Legacy of a Militarized Economy* (Washington, D.C.: Brookings, 1996), pp. 1–66.

6. Robert Gilpin, *The Political Economy of International Relations* (Princeton, N.J.: Princeton University Press, 1987), pp. 341–47.

7. Samuel P. Huntington, "The U.S.—Decline or Renewal?" *Foreign Affairs* (Winter 1988/89), pp. 76–96.

8. For more important writings on the general subjects of American primacy and power and possible decline, see Eric S. Edelman, *Understanding America's Contested Primacy* (Washington, D.C.: Center for Strategic and Budgetary Assessments, 2010); William C. Wohlforth, "The Stability of a Unipolar World," *International Security,* vol. 24, no. 1 (Summer 1999), pp. 5–41; Michael Mastanduno, "System Maker and Privilege Taker: U.S. Power and the International Political Economy," *World Politics,* vol. 61, no. 1 (January 2009), pp. 121–54; Barry Posen, "Command of the Commons: Military Foundations of U.S. Hegemony," *International Security,* vol. 28, no. 1 (Summer 2003), pp. 5–46; Christopher Layne, "The Unipolar Illusion Revisited: The Coming End of the United States' Unipolar Moment," *International Security,* vol. 31, no. 2 (Fall 2006), pp. 147–72; and Aaron L. Friedberg, "The Strategic Implications of Relative Economic Decline," *Political Science Quarterly,* vol. 104, no. 3 (Fall 1989), pp. 401–31.

9. World Bank, *World Development Report 2010* (Washington, D.C.: 2009), p. 380, available at http://siteresources.worldbank.org/INTWDR2010/Resources/5287678-1226014527953/Statistical-Annex.pdf [accessed October 6, 2010].

10. G. John Ikenberry, *After Victory: Institutions, Strategic Restraint, and*

the Rebuilding of Order after Major Wars (Princeton, N.J.: Princeton University Press, 2001).

11. See for example M. Ayhan Kose and Eswar S. Prasad, *Emerging Markets: Resilience and Growth amid Global Turmoil* (Washington, D.C.: Brookings, 2010), p. 130.

12. Bruce D. Jones, "Largest Minority Shareholder in Global Order LLC: The Changing Balance of Influence and U.S. Strategy," *Foreign Policy Paper No. 25* (Washington, D.C.: Brookings, 2011), p. 3, available at http://www.brookings.edu/papers/2011/03_global_order_jones.aspx [accessed September 12, 2011].

13. Stephen M. Walt, *The Origins of Alliances* (Ithaca, N.Y.: Cornell University Press, 1990). Walt was admittedly more worried about how American power and leadership were viewed around the world when he wrote *Taming American Power* (New York: W. W. Norton and Co., 2006). But even then he did not predict that alliances would be formed against it unless Washington was particularly careless or assertive. See for example pp. 11–12 of the latter book.

14. Michael E. O'Hanlon, *Budgeting for Hard Power: Defense and Security Spending Under Barack Obama* (Washington, D.C.: Brookings, 2009), p. 24; International Institute for Strategic Studies, *The Military Balance 2010* (Oxfordshire, UK: Routledge, 2010), pp. 462–68; and World Bank, *World Development Report 2010* (Washington, D.C.: 2009), pp. 378–80.

15. G. John Ikenberry, *Liberal Leviathan: The Origins, Crisis, and Transformation of the American World Order* (Princeton, N.J.: Princeton University Press, 2011), p. 239, based on data from Brett Ashley Leeds, Jeffrey M. Ritter, Sara McLaughlin Mitchell, and Andrew G. Long, "Alliance Treaty Obligations and Provisions, 1915–1944," *International Interactions,* no. 28 (2002). The Shanghai Cooperation Organization works collaboratively on issues such as counterterrorism but does not include a binding mutual defense clause; see Julie Boland, "Ten Years of the Shanghai Cooperation Organization: A Lost Decade? A Partner for the U.S.?" *21st Century Defense Initiative Paper* (Washington, D.C.: Brookings, 2011), p. 13 (available at www.brookings.edu/papers/2011 [accessed September 1, 2011].

16. Joseph S. Nye, Jr., "The Future of American Power," *Foreign Affairs,*

vol. 89, no. 6 (November/December 2010), pp. 2–12; and Joseph S. Nye, Jr., *The Future of Power* (New York: Public Affairs, 2011), pp. 189–90.

17. Feng Wang, "China's Population Destiny: The Looming Crisis," Washington, D.C., Brookings, September 2010, available at http://www.brookings.edu/articles/2010/09_china_population_wang.aspx [accessed November 8, 2010].

18. National Intelligence Council, *Global Trends 2025: A Transformed World* (Washington, D.C.: 2008), pp. 24–27.

19. On the restraint in Indian military policy, see Stephen P. Cohen and Sunil Dasgupta, *Arming Without Aiming: India's Military Modernization* (Washington, D.C.: Brookings, 2010), pp. 1–28. It is true that some speculate India may soon overtake China as the fastest-growing major new power. But that would be from a much lower base of economic power (roughly one fourth the GDP), and India's improved short-to-medium-term prognosis would come partly at the expense of unfettered population growth that will pose its own major challenges, now and down the road. See "How India's Growth Will Outpace China's," "India's Surprising Economic Miracle," and "A Bumpier but Freer Road," *The Economist,* October 2–8, 2010, pp. 11, 75–77.

20. Fareed Zakaria, *The Post-American World* (New York: W. W. Norton and Co., 2008), pp. 187–88.

21. Gerald Bracey, "Heard the One About the 600,000 Chinese Engineers?," *The Washington Post,* May 21, 2006, available at www.washingtonpost.com/wp-dyn/content/article/2006/05/19/AR2006051901760.html [accessed August 12, 2011].

22. Loren Thompson, "Reversing Industrial Decline: A Role for the Defense Budget," Lexington Institute, Arlington, Va., August 2009, p. 5.

23. Darrell M. West, *Brain Gain: Rethinking U.S. Immigration Policy* (Washington, D.C.: Brookings, 2010), pp. 130–36; and Sean Maloney and Christopher Thomas, "Strengthening U.S. Information Technology," in Michael E. O'Hanlon, ed., *Opportunity 08: Independent Ideas for America's Next President*, 2nd ed. (Washington, D.C.: Brookings, 2008), pp. 380–86.

24. Battelle, "2011 Global R&D Funding Forecast," *R&D Magazine*

(December 2010), p. 4, available at http://www.battelle.org/aboutus/rd/2011.pdf [accessed August 1, 2011].

25. West, *Brain Gain,* p. 129.

26. National Science Board, *Science and Engineering Indicators 2010* (Washington, D.C.: 2010), p. 6-20, available at www.nsf.gov/statistics/seind10/seind10.pdf [accessed August 2, 2011].

27. Klaus Schwab, ed., *The Global Competitiveness Report 2011–2012* (Geneva, Switzerland: World Economic Forum, 2011), p. 15, available at http://www3.weforum.org/docs/WEF_GC_Report_2011-12.pdf [accessed September 12, 2011].

28. International Monetary Fund, *World Economic Outlook* (October 2010), p. 204, available at http://www.imf.org/external/pubs/ft/weo/2010/02/pdf/tables.pdf [accessed October 6, 2010]; and Warren B. Rudman, J. Robert Kerrey, Peter G. Peterson, and Robert Bixby, "Realistic Approaches to Head Off a U.S. Economic Crisis," in Michael E. O'Hanlon, ed., *Opportunity 08: Independent Ideas for America's Next President,* 2nd ed. (Washington, D.C.: Brookings, 2008), pp. 262–63.

29. Antoine van Agtmael, *The Emerging Markets Century: How a New Breed of World-Class Companies Is Overtaking the World* (New York: Free Press, 2007), pp. 9–56.

30. Fareed Zakaria, *The Post-American World* (New York: W. W. Norton and Co., 2008), p. 91.

31. International Organization of Motor Vehicle Manufacturers, "Global Vehicle Manufacturing 2000–2010," Paris, France, 2011, available at oica.net/category/production-statistics/ [accessed August 1, 2011].

32. Shipbuilders' Association of Japan, "Shipbuilding Statistics," Tokyo, Japan, March 2010, available at www.sajn.or.jp/c/statistics/Shipbuilding_Statistics_Mar2010.pdf [accessed November 12, 2010].

33. Ian Bremmer, *The End of the Free Market* (New York: Penguin, 2010), pp. 18–24.

34. Executive Office of the President, *Economic Report of the President 2010* (Washington, D.C.: 2010), Table B-12, available at http://www.gpoaccess.gov/eop/tables10.html [accessed October 8, 2010].

35. Hugh B. Price, Amy Liu, and Rebecca Sohmer, "Pathways to the Middle Class: Ensuring Greater Upward Mobility for All

Americans," in Michael E. O'Hanlon, ed., *Opportunity 08: Independent Ideas for America's Next President*, 2nd ed. (Washington, D.C.: Brookings, 2008), pp. 226–29.

36. Ron Haskins and Isabel V. Sawhill, "Attacking Poverty and Inequality: Reinvigorate the Fight for Greater Opportunity," in O'Hanlon, ed., *Opportunity 08*, p. 213.

37. Jeffrey J. Kuenzi, Christine M. Matthews, and Bonnie F. Mangan, "Science, Technology, Engineering, and Mathematics (STEM) Education Issues and Legislative Options," Washington, D.C., Congressional Research Service, May 22, 2006, p. 1; and World Economic Forum, *The Global Competitiveness Report 2009–2010* (Geneva, Switzerland: 2009), p. 17.

38. Darrell M. West, *Brain Gain: Rethinking U.S. Immigration Policy* (Washington, D.C.: Brookings, 2010), p. 130.

39. Statement of Peter R. Orszag, Director, Congressional Budget Office, "Investing in Infrastructure," Testimony before the U.S. Senate Committee on Finance, July 10, 2008, p. 8.

40. Christopher W. Hoene and Michael A. Pagano, "Research Brief on America's Cities," National League of Cities, Washington, D.C., October 2010, available at www.nlc.org [accessed October 7, 2010]; and "Maryland's Silent Tsunami," *Washington Post*, October 13, 2010, p. A18.

41. Klaus Schwab, ed., *The Global Competitiveness Report 2010–2011* (Geneva, Switzerland: World Economic Forum, 2010), p. 19.

42. John S. Duffield, *Over a Barrel: The Costs of U.S. Foreign Oil Dependence* (Stanford, Calif.: Stanford University Press, 2008), pp. 16–26.

43. See International Monetary Fund, *World Economic Outlook Database 1980–2010* (Washington, D.C.: 2011), available at www .imf.org/external/pubs/ft/weo/2011/01/weodata/index.aspx [accessed August 3, 2011]; and World Bank, *World Development Indicators 1960–1970* (Washington, D.C.: 2011), available at data.worldbank .org/data-catalog/world-development-indicators [accessed August 3, 2011].

44. Office of the Secretary of Defense, "Military and Security Developments Involving the People's Republic of China, 2010," Washington, D.C., Department of Defense, p. 42, available at

www.defense.gov/pubs/pdfs/2010_CMPR_final.pdf [accessed August 15, 2011]; and 2011 edition, available at defense.gov/pubs/pdfs/2011_CMPR_final.pdf [accessed September 30, 2011].

45. John J. Mearsheimer, *The Tragedy of Great Power Politics* (New York: W. W. Norton and Company, 2001), p. 402.

46. See Michael J. Green, *Japan's Reluctant Realism* (New York: Palgrave, 2001); Richard C. Bush, *The Perils of Proximity: China-Japan Security Relations* (Washington, D.C.: Brookings, 2010); Nicholas Khoo, "Fear Factor: Northeast Asian Responses to China's Rise," *Asian Security,* vol. 7, no. 2 (2011), pp. 95–118; National Institute for Defense Studies, *East Asian Strategic Review 2011* (Tokyo: 2011), pp. 4–5; Monika Chansoria, "Rising Dragon: Military Modernization of China's PLA in the 21st Century," *The Journal of East Asian Affairs,* vol. 25, no. 1 (Spring/Summer 2011), pp. 15–58; and Carlyle A. Thayer, "China and Southeast Asia: A Shifting Zone of Interaction," *The Borderlands of Southeast Asia: Geopolitics, Terrorism, and Globalization* (Washington, D.C.: National Defense University, 2011), pp. 235–56.

47. See Hiroshi Hiyama, "Japan Concerned at China's Growing Military Reach," Yahoo.com, September 10, 2010, available at www.yahoo.com [accessed September 10, 2011]; John Pomfret, "U.S. Takes Tougher Stance with China," *Washington Post,* July 30, 2010, p. 1; and Malcolm Cook, Raoul Heinrichs, Rory Medcalf, and Andrew Shearer, *Power and Choice: Asian Security Futures* (Sydney, Australia: Lowy Institute, 2010).

48. See, for example, Elisabeth Bumiller, "General Says Beijing Won't Challenge American Military," *New York Times,* May 19, 2011, p. A3.

49. Michael Wines, "China's Rising Military Officers Harbor Deep Suspicion of U.S.," *International Herald Tribune,* October 8, 2010, p. 1.

50. Bernard D. Cole, "Implications of Improvements in PRC Naval Capabilities: 2000–2010," in Roger Cliff, Phillip C. Saunders, and Scott Harold, eds., *New Opportunities and Challenges for Taiwan's Security* (Santa Monica, Calif.: RAND, 2011), pp. 65–71.

51. Christopher D. Yung and Ross Rustici with Isaac Kardon and Joshua Wiseman, *China's Out of Area Naval Operations: Case Studies,*

Trajectories, Obstacles, and Potential Solutions (Washington, D.C.: National Defense University, 2010), pp. 2, 12–13.

52. See Fareed Zakaria, *The Post-American World* (New York: W. W. Norton, 2008), pp. 122–23; and Richard C. Bush and Michael E. O'Hanlon, *A War Like No Other: The Truth About China's Challenge to America* (New York: John Wiley and Sons, 2007), pp. 10–15.

Chapter Three: Deficits, Debt, and a New U.S. Defense Strategy

1. See, for example, Congressional Budget Office, *The Budget and Economic Outlook: An Update* (Washington, D.C.: August 2010), p. 4.
2. David M. Walker, *Comeback America: Turning the Country Around and Restoring Fiscal Responsibility* (New York: Random House, 2009), p. 22.
3. David M. Smick, *The World Is Curved: Hidden Dangers to the Global Economy* (New York: Portfolio, 2009), pp. 20–60; Klaus Schwab, ed., *The Global Competitiveness Report 2009–2010* (Geneva, Switzerland: World Economic Forum, 2009), p. 22; and Zakaria, *The Post-American World,* pp. 190–201.
4. Erskine B. Bowles and Alan K. Simpson, "A Crisis Merely Postponed," *New York Times,* August 3, 2011, available at http://www.nytimes.com/2011/08/03/opinion/the-debt-crisis-merely -postponed.html?ref=opinion [accessed August 3, 2011].
5. See presentation of William Gale, Senior Fellow, Economic Studies, at Brookings, August 17, 2011, available at www.brookings.edu [accessed August 21, 2011].
6. William A. Galston and Maya MacGuineas, "The Future Is Now: A Balanced Plan to Stabilize Public Debt and Promote Economic Growth," Washington, D.C., Brookings Institution, September 2010, p. 1.
7. Congressional Budget Office, *The Budget and Economic Outlook* (Washington, D.C.: 2011), pp. 11, 20–22.
8. The National Commission on Fiscal Responsibility and Reform, *The Moment of Truth* (Washington, D.C.: The White House, December

2010), pp. 13–15, available at http://www.fiscalcommission.gov/sites/ fiscalcommission.gov/files/documents/TheMomentofTruth12_1_2010 .pdf [accessed August 3, 2011].

9. Congressional Budget Office, *Long-Term Implications of the 2012 Future Years Defense Program* (Washington, D.C.: Congressional Budget Office, 2011), p. vii, available at http://www.cbo.gov/ ftpdocs/122xx/doc12264/06-30-11_FYDP.pdf [accessed August 3, 2011].

10. Executive Office of the President, *Historical Tables, Fiscal Year 2012* (Washington, D.C.: Government Printing Office, 2011), pp. 145–47.

11. See, for example, Mark A. Gunzinger, *Sustaining America's Strategic Advantage in Long-Range Strike* (Washington, D.C.: Center for Strategic and Budgetary Assessments, 2010), pp. xiii–xiv; Robert M. Gates, "Helping Others Defend Themselves," *Foreign Affairs,* vol. 89, no. 3 (May/June 2010); and Robert Martinage, *Special Operations Forces: Future Challenges and Opportunities* (Washington, D.C.: Center for Strategic and Budgetary Assessments, 2008), pp. xiii–xvi.

12. Bruce Riedel, "Zawahiri's First 100 Days," *The Daily Beast,* August 15, 2011, available at http://www.brookings.edu/opinions/2011/0815_ zawahiri_riedel.aspx [accessed August 19, 2011].

13. For two analysts advocating stronger possible responses, see Ariel Cohen and Robert E. Hamilton, *The Russian Military and the Georgia War: Lessons and Implications* (Carlisle, Pa.: Strategic Studies Institute, 2011), p. vii.

14. For a good statement of the status of Russian military doctrine and military capabilities, see Stephen J. Blank, " 'No Need to Threaten Us, We Are Frightened of Ourselves': Russia's Blueprint for a Police State, the New Security Strategy," in Stephen J. Blank and Richard Weitz, eds., *The Russian Military Today and Tomorrow* (Carlisle, Pa.: Strategic Studies Institute, 2010), pp. 101–29; and Marcel de Haas, "Russia's Military Doctrine Development," in Stephen J. Blank, ed., *Russian Military Politics and Russia's 2010 Defense Doctrine* (Carlisle, Pa.: Strategic Studies Institute, 2011), pp. 40–55. See also James M. Goldgeier, *The Future of NATO* (New York: Council on Foreign Relations, 2010), pp. 10–13; and address of Assistant Secretary of State Philip Gordon on the New U.S. Approach to Russia, German Marshall Fund, Washington, D.C., June 18, 2010,

available at www.america.gov/st/texttrans-english/2010/June/2010061
8132043SBlebahCO.6471478.html#ixzz0rVNFp9C5 [accessed July 1,
2011].

15. Igor Danchenko, Erica Downs, and Fiona Hill, "One Step Forward,
Two Steps Back?: The Realities of a Rising China and Implications
for Russia's Energy Ambitions," *Foreign Policy Paper No. 22* (August
2010).

16. U.S. Energy Information Administration, "International Energy
Outlook 2010," Department of Energy, Washington, D.C., July 2010,
pp. 30–37, available at www.eia.doe.gov/oiaf/ieo [accessed August 15,
2011].

17. David B. Sandalow, *Freedom from Oil: How the Next President Can
End the United States' Oil Addiction* (New York: McGraw Hill,
2008), p. 18; and Saurin D. Shah, "Electrification of Transport and
Oil Displacement: How Plug-Ins Could Lead to a 50 Percent
Reduction in U.S. Demand for Oil," in David B. Sandalow, ed.,
Plug-In Electric Vehicles: What Role for Washington? (Washington,
D.C.: Brookings, 2009), pp. 22–44.

18. International Institute for Strategic Studies, *The Military Balance
2000–2001* (Oxford, UK: Oxford University Press, 2000), p. 299;
International Institute for Strategic Studies, *The Military Balance
2011* (Oxfordshire, UK: Routledge, 2011), p. 473; and International
Monetary Fund, *World Economic Outlook Database 1980–2010*
(Washington, D.C.: 2011), available at www.imf.org/external/pubs/ft/
weo/2011/01/weodata/index.aspx [accessed August 1, 2011].

19. See for example, Cindy Williams, "Introduction," in Cindy Williams,
ed., *Holding the Line: U.S. Defense Alternatives for the Early 21st
Century* (Cambridge, Mass.: MIT Press, 2001), pp. 7–8; see also
Alain C. Enthoven and K. Wayne Smith, *How Much Is Enough?:
Shaping the Defense Program, 1961–1969* (Santa Monica, Calif.:
RAND, 2005, original publication date 1971), pp. 73–100.

Chapter Four: Tightening Belts at the Pentagon

1. Marcus Weisgerber and Kate Brannen, "Gates Details $13.6 Billion
in DoD Cuts," *Defense News,* March 21, 2011, p. 1, available at
www.defensenews.com.

2. Bruce Newsome, *Made, Not Born: Why Some Soldiers Are Better Than Others* (Westport, Conn.: Praeger, 2007). Some changes are already being made to reduce training modestly; see "Operational Training Rates," *Air Force Magazine* (April 2011), p. 69.

3. For a review of studies on this subject, see Carla Tighe Murray, *Evaluating Military Compensation* (Washington, D.C.: Congressional Budget Office, 2007).

4. For a similar type of list, see Stephen J. Hadley and William J. Perry, Co-Chairmen, "The QDR in Perspective: Meeting America's National Security Needs in the 21st Century," Washington, D.C., Quadrennial Defense Review Independent Panel, 2010, pp. 67–79, available at www.usip.org/files/qdr/qdrreport.pdf [accessed October 20, 2010].

5. For related views from the Defense Business Board, see John T. Burnett, "Panel: DoD Should Cut 111,000 Civilian Jobs," *Federal Times,* July 26, 2010, p. 1.

6. Cindy Williams, "Holding the Line on Infrastructure Spending," in Cindy Williams, ed., *Holding the Line: U.S. Defense Alternatives for the Early 21st Century* (Cambridge, Mass.: Harvard University, 2001), pp. 68–71.

7. On cost savings estimates, see Congressional Budget Office, *Budget Options* (Washington, D.C., 2009), pp. 24–25, available at www.cbo.gov/ftpdocs/102xx/doc10294/08-06-BudgetOptions.pdf [accessed October 20, 2010].

8. Ibid., pp. 28–29.

9. See Secretary of Defense Robert M. Gates, Remarks at American Enterprise Institute, May 24, 2011, available at www.aei.org [accessed August 1, 2011]; Congressional Budget Office, *The Effects of Proposals to Increase Cost-Sharing in TRICARE* (Washington, D.C.: 2009), p. 4.

10. Defense Business Board, "Modernizing the Military Retirement System," July 21, 2011, p. 18, available at http://www.slideshare.net/BrianLucke/modernizing-the-military-retirement-system [accessed August 5, 2011].

Chapter Five: A Smaller Ground Combat Force

1. Office of the Under Secretary of Defense (Comptroller), *National Defense Budget Estimates for 2012* (Washington, D.C.: Department of Defense, 2011), p. 232, available at http://comptroller.defense.gov/ defbudget/fy2012/FY12_Green_Book.pdf [accessed September 9, 2011].

2. For a similar argument see Sustainable Defense Task Force, "Debt, Deficits, and Defense: A Way Forward," available at www.comw.org/ pda/fulltext/1006SDTFreport.pdf [accessed September 15, 2010], p. vii.

3. See for example, Frederick W. Kagan, *Finding the Target: The Transformation of American Military Policy* (New York: Encounter Books, 2006), pp. 180–97, 222–36, 281–86.

4. International Institute for Strategic Studies, *The Military Balance 2010* (Oxfordshire, UK: Routledge, 2010), pp. 32–38.

5. International Institute for Strategic Studies, *The Military Balance 2000* (Oxford, UK: Oxford University Press, 2000), pp. 26–30.

6. Secretary of Defense Robert Gates, *Quadrennial Defense Review Report* (Washington, D.C.: Department of Defense, February 2010), p. 46.

7. For discussions of the force-sizing debates in this period, see for example Kagan, *Finding the Target*, pp. 196–97, 281–86; and Michael E. O'Hanlon, *Defense Policy Choices for the Bush Administration*, 2nd ed. (Washington, D.C.: Brookings, 2002), pp. 9–17, 63–71.

8. Gates, *Quadrennial Defense Review Report*, p. vi.

9. See, for example, Richard L. Kugler, *New Directions in U.S. National Security Strategy, Defense Plans, and Diplomacy* (Washington, D.C.: National Defense University, 2011), pp. 30–33.

10. Robert P. Haffa, Jr., *Rational Methods, Prudent Choices: Planning U.S. Forces* (Washington, D.C.: National Defense University, 1988), pp. 77–82, 110–26; Alain C. Enthoven and K. Wayne Smith, *How Much Is Enough?: Shaping the Defense Program 1961–1969* (Santa Monica, Calif.: RAND, 2005, original publication date 1971), pp. 214–16; John Lewis Gaddis, *Strategies of Containment* (Oxford, UK: Oxford University Press, 1982), pp. 297, 323.

11. John A. Nagl and Travis Sharp, "Operational for What?: The Future

of the Guard and Reserves," *Joint Force Quarterly,* issue 59 (4th Quarter, 2010), pp. 21–29; and Paul McHale, "Unreserved Support," *The American Interest* (September/October 2010), pp. 44–49.

12. See, for example, Secretary of Defense Les Aspin, *Report on the Bottom-Up Review* (Washington, D.C: Department of Defense, 1993), pp. 12–20; Thomas Donnelly, *Operation Iraqi Freedom: A Strategic Assessment* (Washington, D.C.: American Enterprise Institute, 2004), pp. 32–51; Anthony H. Cordesman, *The Iraq War: Strategy, Tactics, and Military Lessons* (Washington, D.C.: CSIS, 2006), pp. 37–40; Michael R. Gordon and General Bernard E. Trainor, *Cobra II: The Inside Story of the Invasion and Occupation of Iraq* (New York: Pantheon Books, 2006), pp. 38–54; and Don Oberdorfer, *The Two Koreas: A Contemporary History* (Reading, Mass.: Addison-Wesley, 1997), p. 315.

13. See Andrew F. Krepinevich, *The Quadrennial Defense Review: Rethinking the U.S. Military Posture* (Washington, D.C.: Center for Strategic and Budgetary Assessments, 2005), pp. 63–65; Michael O'Hanlon, *Defense Strategy for the Post-Saddam Era* (Washington, D.C.: Brookings, 2005), pp. 95–118; and Michael O'Hanlon, *Dealing with the Collapse of a Nuclear-Armed State: The Cases of North Korea and Pakistan* (Princeton, N.J.: Princeton Project on National Security, 2006).

14. Bruce E. Bechtol, Jr., *Defiant Failed State: The North Korean Threat to International Security* (Dulles, Va.: Potomac Books, 2010), pp. 45–47, 186–88.

15. See, for example, International Institute for Strategic Studies, *North Korean Security Challenges: A Net Assessment* (London: International Institute for Strategic Studies, 2011), pp. 47–64.

16. Kenneth M. Pollack, Daniel L. Byman, Martin Indyk, Suzanne Maloney, Michael E. O'Hanlon, and Bruce Riedel, *Which Path to Persia: Options for a New American Strategy Toward Iran* (Washington, D.C.: Brookings, 2009), pp. 94–98.

17. See Stephen Philip Cohen, *The Idea of Pakistan* (Washington, D.C.: Brookings, 2004), pp. 97–130.

18. See International Crisis Group, *Unfulfilled Promises: Pakistan's Failure to Tackle Extremism* (Brussels, 2004).

19. International Institute for Strategic Studies, *The Military Balance 2003–2004*, pp. 140–42.

20. See Bruce Riedel, *Deadly Embrace* (Washington, D.C.: Brookings, 2011).

21. See Sumit Ganguly, *Conflict Unending: India-Pakistan Tensions Since 1947* (New York: Columbia University Press, 2001).

22. International Institute for Strategic Studies, *The Military Balance 2011* (Oxfordshire, UK: Routledge, 2011), p. 472; International Institute for Strategic Studies, *The Military Balance 2001–2002* (Oxford, UK: Oxford University Press, 2001), p. 299; and International Institute for Strategic Studies, *The Military Balance 1991–1992* (London: Brassey's, 1991), p. 212.

23. Thom Shanker, "Defense Secretary Warns NATO of 'Dim' Future," *New York Times,* June 10, 2011, available at www.nytimes .com/2011/06/11/world/europe/11gates.html?_r=1&emc=eta1 [accessed August 1, 2011].

24. As one example, see Choe Sang-Hun, "Island's Naval Base Stirs Opposition in South Korea," *New York Times,* August 19, 2011, available at http://www.nytimes.com/2011/08/19/world/asia/19base. html?_r=1&emc=eta1 [accessed August 19, 2011].

Chapter Six: Global Basing and Global Presence

1. See, for example, Mark Thompson, "$1 Trillion to Spare," *Time,* vol. 177, no. 16 (April 25, 2011), p. 27.

2. See Aaron L. Friedberg, *A Contest for Supremacy: China, America, and the Struggle for Mastery in Asia* (New York: W. W. Norton and Co., 2011).

3. Center on International Cooperation, *Annual Review of Global Peace Operations 2011* (London: Lynne Rienner, 2011), pp. 4, 109, 146.

4. Michael O'Hanlon, "Restructuring U.S. Forces and Bases in Japan," in Mike Mochizuki, ed., *Toward a True Alliance* (Washington, D.C.: Brookings, 1997), p. 161.

5. See Department of Defense, "Department of Defense Active Duty Military Personnel Strengths by Regional Area and by Country,"

March 31, 2011, available at siadapp.dmdc.osd.mil [accessed August 8, 2011].

6. Andrew S. Erickson, Walter C. Ladwig III, and Justin D. Mikolay, "Diego Garcia and the United States' Emerging Indian Ocean Strategy," *Asian Security,* vol. 6, no. 3 (2010), pp. 214–37.

7. Posture Statement of General Douglas M. Fraser, Commander, U.S. Southern Command, before the House Armed Services Committee, March 30, 2011, pp. 17–18, available at southcom.mil/AppsSC/files/634370842750468750.pd6 [accessed August 8, 2011].

8. One modest change to date is in Europe, where the Obama administration plans to keep three Army brigades rather than a smaller number. See Thom Shanker, "U.S. to Keep Three Brigades in Europe," *New York Times,* April 9, 2011, p. A5.

9. Frances Lussier, *Options for Changing the Army's Overseas Basing* (Washington, D.C.: Congressional Budget Office, May 2004), pp. 52, 54; *Strengthening U.S. Global Posture,* p. 13; and General Accounting Office, *DoD's Overseas Infrastructure Master Plans Continue to Evolve,* GAO-06-913R (August 22, 2006), p. 15.

10. Government Accountability Office, "Defense Management: Comprehensive Cost Information and Analysis of Alternatives Needed to Assess Military Posture in Asia," Washington, D.C., May 2011, available at www.gao.gov/new.items/d11316.pdf [accessed August 1, 2011].

11. See Statement of General James F. Amos before the House Armed Services Committee on the 2011 Posture of the United States Marine Corps, March 1, 2011, p. 13, available at http://armedservices.house.gov/index.cfm/files/serve?File_id=6e6d479e-0bea-41a1-8f3d-44b3147640fe [accessed August 10, 2011].

12. Statement of Admiral Gary Roughead, Chief of Naval Operations, before the House Armed Services Committee, March 1, 2011, pp. 3–5, available at navy.mil/navydata/people/cno/Roughead/Testimony/CNO%20Roughead_Testimony_030111.pdf [accessed August 6, 2011].

13. Lussier, *Options for Changing the Army's Overseas Basing*, p. xiv.

14. Michael E. O'Hanlon, *Budgeting for Hard Power* (Washington, D.C.: Brookings, 2009), p. 94.

15. See Eric J. Labs, *Crew Rotation in the Navy: The Long-Term Effect*

on *Forward Presence* (Washington, D.C.: Congressional Budget Office, October 2007), p. 17; Ronald O'Rourke, "Naval Forward Deployments and the Size of the Navy," Congressional Research Service, November 1992, pp. 13–23; and William F. Morgan, *Rotate Crews, Not Ships* (Alexandria, Va.: Center for Naval Analyses, June 1994), pp. 1–9.

16. Labs, *Crew Rotation in the Navy*, pp. 7–14.

17. Sam Lagrone, "USN Relying on 'Cannibalisation' to Stay Afloat," *Jane's Defence Weekly*, July 27, 2011, p. 8.

18. On Russia's interests, see Marlene Laruelle, "Russian Military Presence in the High North: Projection of Power and Capacities of Action," in Stephen J. Blank, ed., *Russia in the Arctic* (Carlisle, Pa.: Strategic Studies Institute, 2011), pp. 63–89.

19. The Sustainable Defense Task Force concurs; see Joshua Stewart, "U.S. Budget Debate Could Cost a Carrier," *Defense News*, August 8, 2011, p. 3.

20. With the fleet response program, the Navy no longer insists on scrupulously maintaining an absolutely continuous presence in the Mediterranean, Persian Gulf, and western Pacific regions. Now it is more inclined to make deployments unpredictable, sometimes using more and sometimes fewer assets than before.

21. Eric J. Labs, *Increasing the Mission Capability of the Attack Submarine Force* (Washington, D.C.: Congressional Budget Office, 2002), pp. xvii, 11–13.

22. Al Cornella, Anthony A. Less, H. G. Taylor, Lewis Curtis, Keith Martin, and James A. Thomson, *Overseas Basing Commission* (Arlington, Va.: Commission on Review of Overseas Military Facility Structure of the United States, May 2005), p. 28.

23. See, for example, O'Rourke, "Naval Forward Deployments and the Size of the Navy," pp. 13–23; and Morgan, *Rotate Crews, Not Ships*, pp. 1–9.

24. O'Hanlon, "Restructuring U.S. Forces and Bases in Japan," in Mochizuki, ed., *Toward a True Alliance*, pp. 171–72.

Chapter Seven: Equipping and
Modernizing the Force

1. P. W. Singer, "Think Before You Cut," ForeignPolicy.com, August 11, 2011, available at www.foreignpolicy.com [accessed August 13, 2011].

2. R. William Thomas, *The Economic Effects of Reduced Defense Spending* (Washington, D.C.: Congressional Budget Office, 1992), pp. 5–42.

3. Briefing by Robert H. Trice, Senior Vice President, Lockheed Martin, "The Business of Aerospace and Defense," Washington, D.C., September 2010, p. 8.

4. Barry D. Watts, *The U.S. Defense Industrial Base: Past, Present and Future* (Washington, D.C.: Center for Strategic and Budgetary Assessments, 2008), pp. 32, 81–90.

5. Aerospace Industries Association, "The Unseen Cost: Industrial Base Consequences of Defense Strategy Choices," Arlington, Va., July 2009, p. 1.

6. Stephen J. Hadley and William J. Perry, Co-Chairmen, "The QDR in Perspective: Meeting America's National Security Needs in the 21st Century," Washington, D.C., Quadrennial Defense Review Independent Panel, 2010, pp. 84–91, available at www.usip.org/files/qdr/qdrreport.pdf [accessed October 20, 2010].

7. Over the last half century, expressed in constant 2010 dollars, acquisition budgets have averaged about $150 billion a year, with the RDT&E budget about $50 billion of that total on average. Watts, *The U.S. Defense Industrial Base,* pp. 21–28.

8. See Department of Defense, "Selected Acquisition Report (SAR) Summary Tables," December 31, 2010, available at www.acq.osd.mil/ara/am/sar/SST-2010-12.pdf [accessed August 10, 2011], pp. 1–23.

9. M. Thomas Davis and Nathaniel C. Fick, "America's Endangered Arsenal of Democracy," *Joint Forces Quarterly,* issue 62 (3rd quarter, 2011), p. 94.

10. See Lane Pierrot, *A Look at Tomorrow's Tactical Air Forces* (Washington, D.C.: Congressional Budget Office, 1997); and R. William Thomas, *Effects of Weapons Procurement Stretch-Outs on Costs and Schedules* (Washington, D.C.: Congressional Budget Office, 1987).

11. Michael E. O'Hanlon, *The Science of War* (Princeton, N.J.: Princeton University Press, 2009), pp. 8–31; and Amy Belasco, *Paying for Military Readiness and Upkeep: Trends in Operation and Maintenance Spending* (Washington, D.C.: Congressional Budget Office, 1997), pp. 5–15.

12. Hadley and Perry, "The QDR in Perspective," p. 53.

13. See, for example, Thomas G. Mahnken, "Striving for Balance in Defense," *Proceedings* (June 2010), pp. 36–41, available at www.usni .org [accessed September 5, 2010]; Hadley and Perry, "The QDR in Perspective"; and Jan Van Tol, *AirSea Battle: A Point-of-Departure Operational Concept* (Washington, D.C.: Center for Strategic and Budgetary Assessments, 2010).

14. Statement of Christine H. Fox, Director of Cost Assessment and Program Evaluation, Department of Defense, before the Senate Armed Services Committee, May 19, 2011, available at www.armed -services.senate.gov/e_witnesslist.cfm?id=5213 [accessed August 1, 2011].

15. See Statement of General James F. Amos before the House Armed Services Committee on the 2011 Posture of the United States Marine Corps, March 1, 2011, p. 13, available at http://armedservices.house .gov/index.cfm/files/serve?File_id=6e6d479e-0bea-41a1-8f3d -44b3147640fe [accessed August 10, 2011].

16. John A. Tirpak, "New Life for Old Fighters," *Air Force Magazine* (February 2011), pp. 28–34.

17. Dave Majumdar, "F-35 on Target for Key Goals," *Defense News,* June 20, 2011, p. 1.

18. See Capt. Henry J. Hendicks and Lt. Col. J. Noel Williams, "Twilight of the Superfluous Carrier," *Proceedings* (May 2011), available at www.usni.org [accessed May 3, 2011].

19. See U.S. Air Force, "Fact Sheet on MQ-9 Reaper, 2010," available at http://www.af.mil/information/factsheets/factsheet.asp?id= 6405 [accessed August 13, 2011]; and Congressional Budget Office, *Policy Options for Unmanned Aerial Systems* (Washington, D.C.: June 2011), pp. ix–x, available at www.cbo.gov [accessed August 13, 2011].

20. Leithen Francis, "Mission Impossible," *Aviation Week and Space Technology,* August 15, 2011, p. 27.

21. See P. W. Singer, *Wired for War: The Robotics Revolution and Conflict in the 21st Century* (New York: Penguin Press, 2009); and Michael E. O'Hanlon, *Technological Change and the Future of Warfare* (Washington, D.C.: Brookings, 2000), p. 65.

22. Michael Hoffman, "U.S. Army to Follow Most Advice from Scathing DoD Report," *Defense News,* July 25, 2011, p. 4; and Rear Admiral John D. Butler, "The Sweet Smell of Acquisition Success," *Proceedings* (June 2011), pp. 22–28, available at www.usni.org [accessed August 1, 2011].

23. For a good historical example of such a case, see Montgomery C. Meigs, *Slide Rules and Submarines: American Scientists and Subsurface Warfare in World War II* (Honolulu: University Press of the Pacific, 2002); on the more general challenge of promoting innovation within military bureaucracies, see for example Stephen Peter Rosen, *Winning the Next War* (Ithaca, N.Y.: Cornell University Press, 1991).

24. The Nunn-McCurdy Amendment to the 1982 Defense Authorization Act triggers reviews of weapons when their estimated program cost exceeds by 50 percent original estimates. See Department of Defense, "Selected Acquisition Report (SAR) Summary Tables," Washington, D.C., April 2, 2010, p. 3, available at www.acq.osd.mil/ara/2009%20 DEC%20SAR.pdf [accessed November 12, 2010].

25. For a provocative and insightful, yet to my mind ultimately unconvincing, argument along these lines (making the case that great-power war planning is no longer nearly as important as it once was), see Thomas P. M. Barnett, *The Pentagon's New Map: War and Peace in the Twenty-First Century* (New York: G. P. Putnam's, 2004). I agree with Barnett that great-power wars are unlikely to be waged—but their likelihood can increase to the extent that we fail to prepare for them and thereby fail to deter them.

26. On cost savings estimates, see Congressional Budget Office, *Budget Options* (Washington, D.C.: 2009), pp. 5–21, available at www.cbo .gov/ftpdocs/102xx/doc10294/08-06-BudgetOptions.pdf [accessed October 20, 2010]; Department of Defense, "Selected Acquisition Report (SAR) Summary Tables," Washington, D.C., December 31, 2009, pp. 21–23, available at www.acq.osd.mil/ara/2009%20DEC%20 SAR.pdf [accessed October 20, 2010]; and Michael E. O'Hanlon, *A*

Skeptic's Case for Nuclear Disarmament (Washington, D.C.: Brookings, 2010), pp. 110–31.

27. John P. Caves, Jr., "Avoiding a Crisis of Confidence in the U.S. Nuclear Deterrent," *Strategic Forum No. 252* (January 2010), available at wwwl.ndu.edu/inss.

28. For the cost estimates, see O'Hanlon, *A Skeptic's Case for Nuclear Disarmament*.

29. Congressional Budget Office, *Reducing the Deficit: Spending and Revenue Options* (Washington, D.C.: Congressional Budget Office, 2011), p. 96, available at www.cbo.gov [accessed August 13, 2011].

30. Ibid., p. 90; and Michael E. O'Hanlon, *The Science of War* (Princeton, N.J.: Princeton University Press, 2009), p. 26. On East Asia, and the potential for rivalries and conflicts within, see for example Robert D. Kaplan, *Monsoon: The Indian Ocean and the Future of American Power* (New York: Random House, 2010); Richard C. Bush, *The Perils of Proximity* (Washington, D.C.: Brookings, 2010); and Andrew S. Erickson, Walter C. Ladwig III, and Justin D. Mikolay, "Diego Garcia and the United States' Emerging Indian Ocean Strategy," *Asian Security,* vol. 6, no. 3 (September–December 2010), pp. 214–37.

31. Sam Lagrone, "USN to Go Down to Nine Carrier Strike Groups by Year's End," *Jane's Defence Weekly,* August 17, 2011, p. 9.

32. Eric J. Labs, "An Analysis of the Navy's Fiscal Year 2012 Shipbuilding Plan," Congressional Budget Office, Washington, D.C., June 2011, p. 15, available at www.cbo.gov/ftpdocs/122xx/doc12237/ 06-23-NavyShipbuilding.pdf [accessed August 1, 2011].

33 Commander John Patch, "The Wrong Ship at the Wrong Time," *Proceedings* (January 2011), pp. 16–19, available at www.usni.org [accessed August 1, 2011]; and Lexington Institute, "Countering the Asymmetric Threat from Sea Mines," Alexandria, Virginia, March 2010.

Chapter Eight: Stress Testing the Force with China and Iran

1. For a trenchant analysis and summary of these challenges, see Kenneth G. Lieberthal, *Managing the China Challenge: How to*

Achieve Corporate Success in the People's Republic (Washington, D.C.: Brookings, 2011), pp. 11–47.

2. See, for example, Michael D. Swaine, *America's Challenge: Engaging a Rising China in the Twenty-First Century* (Washington, D.C.: Carnegie Endowment, 2011), pp. 147–82.

3. Keith Bradsher, "Chasing Rare Earths: Foreign Companies Expand in China for Access to Crucial Metals," *New York Times*, August 25, 2011, p. B1.

4. John A. Tirpak, "A Force at Razor's Edge," *Air Force Magazine* (April 2010), p. 26.

5. This estimated capacity for sustained delivery from airlift and sealift together is not to be confused with a metric commonly used for airlift in particular, million ton miles per day (MTM/D). The United States presently has nearly 60 MTM/D of airlift capacity—defined as the sum of all airlifters' payload, times their average speed, times their number of sustainable hours of flight per day, all divided by two to account for the fact that the planes must fly back (more or less) empty to load up again for another trip. See David Arthur, *Options for Strategic Military Transportation Systems* (Washington, D.C.: Congressional Budget Office, September 2005), pp. 8–9.

6. David Fulghum and Bill Sweetman, "Intel About China Flawed: Booming Economy Accelerating China's Military Development," *Aviation Week and Space Technology*, January 10, 2011, pp. 26–27; and Office of the Secretary of Defense, "Military and Security Developments Involving the People's Republic of China," pp. 29–33.

7. Owen R. Cote, Jr., "Assessing the Undersea Balance Between the U.S. and China," MIT Strategic Studies Program, Cambridge, Mass., February 2011, available at http://web.mit.edu/ssp/publications/working_papers/Undersea%20Balance%20WP11-1.pdf [accessed August 1, 2011].

8. On the challenges of dealing with Iran, and the way in which sanctions might be employed or modified, see for example Meghan L. O'Sullivan, "Iran and the Great Sanctions Debate," *Washington Quarterly*, vol. 33, no. 4 (October 2010), pp. 7–21; and Kenneth M. Pollack, "Pariahs in Tehran," *The National Interest*, no. 110 (November/December 2010), pp. 42–52.

9. Caitlin Talmadge, "Closing Time: Assessing the Iranian Threat to the

Strait of Hormuz," *International Security,* vol. 33, no. 1 (Summer 2008), p. 115.

10. Robert D. Kaplan, "A Power Shift in Asia," *Washington Post,* September 25, 2011, p. A17.

Chapter Nine: Intelligence, Homeland Security, Diplomacy, Democracy, and Development

1. Roger Z. George, "Reflections on CIA Analysis: Is It Finished?," *Intelligence and National Security,* vol. 26, no. 1 (February 2011), pp. 72–81.

2. Barton Gellman, "How the G-Man Got His Groove Back," *Time,* May 9, 2011, pp. 22–32.

3. Ken Dilanian, "Overall U.S. Intelligence Budget Tops $80 Billion," *Los Angeles Times,* October 28, 2010, available at http://articles .latimes.com/2010/oct/28/nation/la-na-intel-budget-20101029 [accessed August 15, 2011].

4. Richard K. Betts, *Enemies of Intelligence: Knowledge and Power in American National Security* (New York: Columbia University Press, 2007).

5. Statement of General David H. Petraeus before the Senate Select Committee on Intelligence, June 23, 2011, available at www .intelligence.senate.gov/110623/statement.pdf [accessed August 15, 2011].

6. Deputy Secretary of Defense William J. Lynn III, "A Military Strategy for the New Space Environment," *Washington Quarterly*, vol. 34, no. 3 (Summer 2011), pp. 10–12.

7. See Dana Priest and William M. Arkin, "A Hidden World, Growing Beyond Control," *Washington Post,* July 19, 2010, available at http:// projects.washingtonpost.com/top-secret-america/ articles/a-hidden-world-growing-beyond-control/print [accessed May 1, 2011].

8. Paul R. Pillar, "Unintelligent Design," *The National Interest* (September/October 2010), pp. 43–50; and Michael V. Hayden, "The State of the Craft: Is Intelligence Reform Working?," *World Affairs* (September/October 2010), pp. 35–47.

9. Clark Kent Ervin, *Open Target: Where America Is Vulnerable to*

Attack (New York: Palgrave, 2006); and Stephen Flynn, *America the Vulnerable: How Our Government Is Failing to Protect Us from Terrorism* (New York: HarperCollins, 2004).

10. Michael E. O'Hanlon, *Budgeting for Hard Power: Defense and Security Spending Under Barack Obama* (Washington, D.C.: Brookings, 2011), pp. 115–25.

11. Steven Radelet, *Emerging Africa: How 17 Countries Are Leading the Way* (Washington, D.C.: Center for Global Development, 2010), pp. 105–6.

12. Hillary Rodham Clinton, "Leading Through Civilian Power," *Foreign Affairs,* vol. 89, no. 6 (November/December 2010), p. 13.